M000029765

# the Groovy Chicks' Road Trip to Peace

# the Groovy Chicks' Road Trip to Peace

## Dena J. Dyer & Laurie Barker Copeland

LIFE JOURNEY®

*Bringing Home the Message for Life*

COOK COMMUNICATIONS MINISTRIES
Colorado Springs, Colorado • Paris, Ontario
KINGSWAY COMMUNICATIONS LTD
Eastbourne, England

Life Journey® is an imprint of
Cook Communications Ministries, Colorado Springs, CO 80918
Cook Communications, Paris, Ontario
Kingsway Communications, Eastbourne, England

THE GROOVY CHICKS' ROAD TRIP TO PEACE
© 2005 by Dena Dyer and Laurie Copeland

All rights reserved. No part of this book may be reproduced without written permission, except for brief quotations in books and critical reviews. For information,
write Cook Communications Ministries, 4050 Lee Vance View, Colorado Springs,
CO 80918.

Cover Design: Sandy Flewelling
Groovy Chicks logo and sidebar graphic: John Copeland and iC MEDiA
PRODUCTiONS

First Printing, 2005
Printed in the United States of America
1 2 3 4 5 6 7 8 9 10 Printing/Year 09 08 07 06 05

Unless otherwise noted, Scripture quotations are taken from the HOLY BIBLE,
NEW INTERNATIONAL VERSION®. Copyright © 1973, 1978, 1984 by
International Bible Society. Used by permission of Zondervan Publishing House.
All rights reserved. Scripture quotations marked NKJV are taken from the New
King James Version®. Copyright © 1982 by Thomas Nelson, Inc. Used by permis-
sion. All rights reserved. Scripture quotations marked NASB are taken from the
NEW AMERICAN STANDARD BIBLE®, Copyright © 1960, 1962, 1963, 1968, 1971,
1972, 1973, 1975, 1977, 1995 by The Lockman Foundation. Used by permission.
Scriptures quotations marked CEV are taken from the Contemporary English
Version © 1995 by American Bible Society. Used by permission. Scripture quota-
tions marked NLT are taken from the Holy Bible. New Living Translation copyright
© 1996 by Tyndale Charitable Trust. Used by permission of Tyndale House
Publishers. Scriptures quotations marked ESV are taken from The Holy Bible,
English Standard Version, copyright © 2001 by Crossway Bibles, a division of
Good News Publishers. Used by permission. All rights reserved. Scripture quotations marked KJV are taken from the King James Version of the Holy Bible. Italics
in Scripture have been added by the authors for emphasis.

Library of Congress Cataloging-in-Publication Data

The groovy chicks' road trip to peace / [edited by] Dena Dyer and Laurie Barker
Copeland.
    p. cm.
  ISBN 0-7814-4150-1 (pbk.)
  1. Christian women--Religious life--Anecdotes. I. Dyer, Dena, 1970- II. Copeland,
Laurie Barker, 1958-
BV4527.G76 2005
248.8'43--dc22
                    2004030386

*For Mom, who is definitely a Groovy Chick.*
*—D.D.*


*For my husband, John, who is mighty Groovy,*
*even if he isn't a Chick.*
*And for my daughter, Kailey,*
*who is the Grooviest Chicklette in my life.*
*—L.B.C.*

# CONTENTS

## PART THREE
## I CAN'T GET NO SATISFACTION (PEACE WITH SELF)

# FOREWORD

GIGI GRAHAM

Groovy ... Ever since this word came into our vocabulary, I have thought it would be nice to be thought of as "groovy." To me that meant you were fun and really "with it."

However, for many years I thought to be groovy was not consistent with what God had in mind when he said a woman with a gentle, quiet spirit was of great worth in his sight. (See 1 Peter 3:4.)

I am a feisty, warmhearted, free spirited, fun loving, energetic, and passionate woman. And I have struggled most of my life with trying to balance my personality with what I perceived as being a gentle, quiet spirit.

As a young woman, I envied those who were naturally more quiet and gentle. They fit my image of a "godly woman" and seemed more peaceful. So obviously, I thought, they must be much more pleasing to God. My personality was often frowned upon by well meaning, but disapproving older saints. I assumed that if they disapproved, so did God. So I struggled and prayed diligently for God to change me.

I became discouraged, because try as I did, I could never seem to attain what I perceived to be the characteristics of a woman who pleased God and gained the approval of other Christians.

After many years of struggle and wasted energy, I began to understand that a gentle, quiet spirit has nothing to do with personality, but rather with our attitude of submission to him. It is a heart issue, not a personality issue. I came to realize and accept the fact that God made me just the way he wanted me to be with the personality he wanted me to have. It was then I discovered a freedom in Christ to be me.

Dena and Laurie have discovered and share in this book what took me years to learn, accept, and now enjoy: freedom in Christ to be all he created us to be, and his peace that comes when we accept the freedom he offers.

Yes, it is possible to be godly and groovy ... so grab on, and enjoy the ride!

GIGI GRAHAM

# Acknowledgments

## From Dena

A Big, Groovy thank-you to

Jesus, my Healer, Savior, Friend, and Lord. Thank you for letting me live my dreams! I am so blessed.

My family (Carey, Jordan, and Jackson), for making sacrifices so I could put this book together.

My parents, my in-laws, and my brother, for your support and encouragement during the lean years before the book contracts came. Thanks for believing in me and not saying, "Why don't you get a real job?"

Laurie, for your willingness to go on this journey with me. I sooo appreciate your humor, attention to detail (who'da thunk it?), tireless work, and great ideas. (And for the great inside jokes we can't share with anyone else!) It was fun, tiring, wonderful, and crazy—a REAL trip!—working together. I'm glad God brought you to Glen Rose for that conference. Who knew where he would take us?!

My girlfriends (and The Ha-Ha Sisterhood)—Laura, Shiloh, Sandi, Wendy, Linda, Tina, Beth, Jan, Carrie, Judy, Kathy, Kim, LaDonna, and Deanna—for helping me laugh and stay positive in the midst of a very stressful year.

Tom and Sandi—for encouraging me to do something literary with "Starshine." You guys are awesome!

Russ Hearn and the crew at the Granbury Live theater in Granbury, Texas—for creating the Starshine character and letting me run with it!

## From Laurie

"I'd like to thank the following people for this award ..."

Since this is the very first book I've written, I feel like a newbie actress accepting her first Academy Award. Get out the Kleenex and set the timer....

A very talented group of people diligently helped me hone the craft of writing. Thanks to Eva Marie Everson, the Word Weaver's Critique Group, and the UgoGirls: Tama, Julie, Rhonda, and Gloria.

Dena, my writing partner and fellow Groovy Chick. From our first meeting in Texas to that now famous (at least in our minds!) e-mail where you said, "What do you think about a book on a couple of Groovy Chicks?" our working together was ordained and action-packed, to say the least! I thank God for you!

I am so blessed to have many giving people who prayed for this stuttering Moses as I entered into the scary but promising new land: my mom and dad, who have prayed for me since before day one; my brothers and their families; Granny; my Groovy Chick girlfriends who brainstormed, listened, and prayed for me: Cheri, Liz, Denise, Christie, Debbie, Mary, Julie, Laura, and Susan; my loyal prayer warriors: Alma, Carole Suzanne, Cathy, Dean, Diane, Dina, Donna, Kelly, Janet, Karen, Linda Lee, Lori, Marilyn, Michelle, Olga, Pat, Steve, Ron, Greg, Rozie, Tami, and Tammy; Bill Pickett, who always believed in me, and the women of Pine Castle; and my Sunday night home group, who prayed for me when I had just "a stirring." And oh yes, to Sherry and Ruthie, whose "Rosie and Sadie" characters taught me that dressing up and acting silly could be loads of fun. Pepper thanks you.

These acknowledgments would not be complete without thanking the three most important, loving (and tolerant!) people in my life: my husband, John, my li'l Chicklette daughter, Kailey, and my Lord and Savior, the Prince of Peace ... the One to whom we give all the glory. It's because of him that we are Groovy.

## FROM BOTH OF US

To CLASS and the Littauers ... for your training and mentoring. You "let it begin in me!"

To Mary McNeil, our editor, thanks for believing in us and making it happen!

To our agent, Frank Weimann of the Literary Group and to Steve Laube, who saw the vision for this project from the beginning, for taking a chance on two new authors—it gave us a real confidence boost!

To John Copeland and iC MEDiA PRODUCTiONS, for our Groovy Chicks logo and sidebar graphics.

To Allison Gappa Bottke, for her support, advice, and encouragement.

To all the people who submitted your Groovy tales to us: we loved your stories and wish we could have used each one.

To our contributors, for being patient with this first road trip. We are so blessed to have your life experiences as part of our project! You guys rock!

# INTRODUCTION

## DENA'S STORY

I'm writing this in a hot house during August in Texas. (It's a good thing we Lone Star State gals "glisten" instead of sweat.) Why the perspiration? Well, my air conditioner broke just as our book deadline approached.

When my husband told me the bad news about our favorite appliance, I was not amused. "Lord," I moaned, "if everything is a test, like Rick Warren says in *The Purpose-Driven Life®*, I think I'm failing!" (I also added a little prayer and asked that this book sell as well as that one. We'll see.)

Take my word for it—writing a book about peace is like praying for patience: you don't want to do it unless you have to!

In the year we've been working on this compilation, I've experienced a difficult pregnancy; a job change; a longer-than-expected hospital stay to have the baby (who came six weeks early); problems with both our vehicles; difficulties with hot water heaters, refrigerators, and leaky pipes; and adjustment problems with our firstborn as he adapted to his new little brother.

I thank God that most of the trials were temporary—and that all of them turned out fine. I have so much to be thankful for! Though I'm sometimes stressed, I'm extremely blessed.

So believe me, I am writing as a fellow struggler, not as an expert with all the answers. I definitely need God's peace to invade my chaotic world on a daily, if not hourly, basis.

And that's why I asked Laurie to coauthor a book about Groovy Chicks—so we could encourage other women in their journeys through a world spinning out of control. I've discovered—mostly by trying (and failing) to find peace in other places—that Jesus is the only way I'll ever find lasting peace.

## LAURIE'S STORY

"A book on *what?*" I asked, wondering if I'd understood my writing buddy correctly.

"Peace," Dena said, her voice soft as though trying not to scare a wild and fragile kitten.

Feeling like Butterfly McQueen in *Gone with the Wind*, I immediately said, "But I don't know *nuthin'* about peace!"

But before I could take another protesting breath, I felt a breath of a different kind go through me ... one of, yes ... peace. God was reassuring me that the fact that I *felt* "peace-challenged" was *exactly* why we were doing a book on the subject.

It's funny, but I've discovered that I learn about a subject while I write about it. When my thoughts pour out on the page, I find the answers to nagging questions like, "Why can't I be a size three?" and "Why do I let fear rob me of so many things?" and "Why can't my yard look like the ones on *Curb Appeal?*"

And in the writing of this book, I made a tremendous discovery: I've had it wrong all these years. I've always thought I wasn't a peaceful person, but I am! Here's the reason: there is a big difference between contentment and peace. My lack of satisfaction is a contentment issue. *Peace* is knowing and believing the foundational truth that no matter the circumstance, God is in control of what happens in your life.

Charles Stanley put it this way: "Peace is an inner quality that flows out of a right relationship with God.... It is precisely in the 'going-through' stage of any crisis that God's peace is most clearly manifested to all." (*Finding Peace: God's Promise of a Life Free from Regret, Anxiety, and Fear,* Thomas Nelson, 2003, 22–23.)

And Paul, while in prison, wrote, "The peace of God, which surpasses all understanding, will guard your hearts and minds in Christ Jesus" (Phil. 4:7 ESV). I'd been reading this verse for years, when suddenly I got it—I'm not *supposed* to understand peace because it surpasses *all understanding*! That sure takes a load off my mind.

## GROOVY CHICKS, UNITE!

Remember the sixties and seventies, when bell-bottom-clad hippies held up two fingers and said, "Peace, man"? Drugs, free love, and a controversial war made headlines during that tumultuous period. Just take a look around our planet, and you'll realize things haven't changed much. The world wanted peace then, and we long for it still. But the only answer to peace has been—and always will be—Jesus Christ.

That's where the Groovy Chicks, Pepper and Starshine, come in. These two wacky, Jesus-loving hippies are the original Groovy Chicks (they're also our alter egos, but don't tell anyone). Starshine and Pepper were born out of our desire to combine speaking, acting, singing, writing, and ministering to women into one Groovalicious package.

## Just What Is a Groovy Chick?

The Top 10 Qualities of a Groovy Chick—

10. You love to laugh (especially at yourself!) and see life as a celebration.
9. You know that God cares more about the size of your heart than the size of your jeans.
8. Your wardrobe, accessories, and home decor reflect the real you.
7. You can multitask with the best of them, but you also know the Proverbs 31 woman didn't do it all in one day.
6. You carve out moments in your busy schedule to spend time with friends and family.
5. You have trouble resisting a bargain, sweet baby, or cute puppy.
4. Your car may be messy, but it's only because you're the carpool/soccer/mission trip Volunteer Queen.
3. You appreciate old age, especially if it's staring you in the face.
2. You're not a pacifist, but are passionate about life.

And the #1 quality of a Groovy Chick is ...

1. You know you are Groovy only because of Christ in you!

Without Jesus, we would be, as Shakespeare said, "full of sound and fury, signifying nothing" (*MacBeth*, Act 5, Scene 5). But *with* Christ in our lives, we can be very Groovy, indeed.

Just listen to what *The Message* says in Psalm 18:30:

> What a God! His road
>> stretches straight and smooth.
> Every GOD-direction is road-tested.
>> Everyone who runs toward him
> Makes it.

And who better to take you on the road than two crazy, God-fearing hippies? So pack your bags and hop into our VW bus!

## NAVIGATION AIDS ON THE ROAD TRIP

You'll notice that along with every story, there's a little bonus or two from Dena (Starshine) or Laurie (Pepper). We hope these sidebars will further encourage you on your road trip to peace.

*Pepper's Pit Stops* are road trip guides for the weary or misguided. Or, they might just be really Groovy ideas.

*Starshine's Smile Markers* are quotes to inspire you or make you laugh out loud.

*Pepper's Offramps* are offbeat road trip exits. Get ready for some really weird stuff, just for the fun of it!

*Starshine's How's Your InnerState?* are thought-provoking questions and journaling prompts. (Do not attempt to do the journaling while driving!)

*Lost? Try GPS (God's Positioning System)* are verses on peace straight from the Source—God's Word.

Well, that's it. Now fasten your seatbelts, grab some snacks, and join Pepper, Starshine, and a bunch of their Groovy friends on a road trip to peace—peace with God, peace with others, and peace with ourselves.

## PART ONE

# FEELING GROOVY
# (Peace with God)

# Shoulder Pads and Insecurities: Slip Slidin' Away

Laurie Barker Copeland

It's simple," my friend said. "You just sign up on the Web, and you'll find out how our friends from high school are doing!"

Strangely, twenty-five years this side of graduation, it sounded fun. What was I *thinking*?!

My post-high school world crumbled when my first Internet contact came from Rick, an old boyfriend. We had dated when he was the soccer team captain and I was a perky cheerleader.

And now? Now my little *toe* couldn't fit in those hip-hugging, patch-adorned bell-bottoms I used to wear.

Get the picture?

Not many days after that, the phone rang and ... it was him!

"It's so nice to hear from you, Rick," I lied. "Oh? You're coming to town? Yes, I would *love* to see you and meet your family! When? Next month?!"

(Dear Lord, open the earth and swallow me up now!) "Sure!" NOT!

Please understand I wasn't panicking because he was my

old boyfriend. And I did want to see him. I just didn't want *him* to see *me*.

As I hung up the phone, I wondered how much weight I could lose in one month if I stopped eating altogether.

I'm acutely aware that in many people's minds, being overweight is a sign of failure. God had spent many long hours with me, convincing me to put my trust in him and not other people's opinions of me. Only recently had I learned about letting go and letting God, as the old saying goes. At the time of Rick's call, I was happily kicking insecurity's invisible fanny out of my life.

Now, I looked in the mirror to see if the situation warranted panic. Insecurity's miserable face stared back at me.

"Rick isn't even going to recognize me!" I said to no one in particular. "He's going to be embarrassed that he ever dated me.... He and his family will never get to know the real me in such a short visit...."

On and on it went. However, my thoroughly unjealous loves-me-just-as-I-am husband, John, felt totally comfortable with the whole situation.

Over time, I began to think, *Y'know, I was a cheerleader and I gained this much weight. Maybe he's gained some, too, and we can just have a good laugh about it.*

That idea evaporated the day that photos of his family arrived via cyberspace. The snapshots revealed a beautiful wife and daughter, a football player son, and a Rick who was still playing soccer ... and was still a hunk.

Rah ... rah ... rah ... sis ... boom ... Waah!

I warned him on the phone. "I'm not the person I used to be," I said nervously. He chuckled reassuringly and said, "None of us is."

Ha! Easy for *him* to say!

The dreaded day arrived, and I hadn't lost an ounce. When it came time to get dressed, I turned to my fashion-conscious daughter, Kailey, for help.

Pulling outfit after outfit out of my closet, I asked, "Which one makes me look best?"

All the while, I searched for a way to explain to my ten-year-old how hard it is to meet with old friends who might think you're a failure because you haven't "preserved" well.

We finally settled on a lime green silk blouse and slenderizing black pants. I knew that shoulder pads were "out," but I decided the blouse needed them. Those little rescuers riding on my shoulders helped to counterbalance my hips!

When we met Rick and his family in a local restaurant, as expected, Rick looked right through me, never imagining I was his former sweetheart. But after I waved him down and we had a good laugh, Rick introduced me to his boffo family.

After being seated, we entered into lively conversation. For some unexplainable reason, normally independent Kailey chose this moment to cling to me. She rested both hands on my shoulder and then stroked them down along my arms. After repeating this exercise many times, it felt as though my blouse was twisted in five or six directions.

I decided it was time to check on those shoulder pads. I casually draped my right hand on my left shoulder, Garbo style. *It wasn't there!* I moved my hand ever so discreetly down my arm. *It wasn't there, either!*

*Rats!* I began to panic. *It's probably sticking out of my neckline!*

Keeping eye contact and stroking my chin as though intensely interested in the upbeat conversation happening a mere two feet away, I slowly moved my fingertips across my V-neckline.

*It's ... not ... there!* I tried to control the creeping panic rising within. *Where could it be?!... No ... it couldn't be....* I knew I had to check, but how could I without being noticed? The oldies tune flashed across my mind: "Slip slidin' away...."

I stole a glance down at my chest. There was the renegade shoulder pad—stretched across my left bosom like a two-inch thick, super-sized Band-Aid!

Oh, to be invisible! I knew I couldn't just stand up and dash out. I patiently waited for a lull in the conversation, my hand searching my face for a bump, a mole, *anything* to pick at, so my arm would cover my Band-Aided bosom.

At last, the lull arrived, and I nonchalantly sashayed to the bathroom. I picked up speed the closer I got to the ladies room.

Bursting through the door, I hurried to the mirror to study my form. Yup, there it appeared. One side of my bosom was an entire Sears catalog-width larger than the other. I began to giggle, which turned into a snort and then a belly laugh.

With gusto, I reached inside my blouse, yanked the perpetrator out and slam-dunked it into File Thirteen. With pleasure!

And I enjoyed the rest of my evening, even after I had guffawed all my makeup off in the water closet.

Why is it that though I am happily married and a confident, contributing member of society, I could so quickly turn into a half-wit when an old friend showed up? I reverted to a silly schoolgirl, overly concerned with such a temporal thing as looks.

This is not to say I am championing a new ban on shoulder pads or anything else that makes us look better. As my loving brother always says, "If the barn needs painting, paint it!"

However, I *am* championing the goal of putting our confidence and our trust completely in God ... and leaving them there!

It's true I am no longer the twelfth-grade cheerleader with

long blonde hair and "abs of steel." It's also true that I am a forty-something woman who has added an entire extra person to my hips, and yes, I don't always have my act together.

But I'm ready to take those "truths" about myself and hand them over to God. I want to experience his peace, his approval, and his perspective on it all. I long to realize and thoroughly accept that I can dare to be me ... *the one and only.*

Doesn't God have a great sense of humor? He revealed my insecurities in the shape of a shoulder pad. What a ridiculous object to plant my security on! Especially when I realize whom I *should* be relying on: my God, the One who makes me truly unique ... just as I am.

With or without shoulder pads.

## Starshine's Smile Markers

Enjoy your life without comparing
it with that of others.
Marquis de Condorcet

**SMILE MARKER**

# GARDEN OF EDEN

MARCEA GALINDO

They called it the Garden of Eden, a swimming hole so breath-taking you'd think it was the real thing. Intrigued, my family decided we had to see it.

So one blistering day, after the morning meetings at Mount Hermon family camp near San Jose, the four of us trudged down the curving hill leading from the camp. At the bottom, we found the path of the train tracks and started out. In the blistering California heat, the only thing that kept us going was the thought of the cool water waiting for us in the lush garden.

We followed the path to the river, but there I stopped in my tracks. The path continued up over the river—*high* over the river. Outwardly, I froze. Inwardly, I screamed in terror. In desperation, I suggested to my family that we cross through the water. Not only was it a ridiculous request, it was also too late. By that time, my vivacious little brother and my dad were already halfway across the trestle. My mom tried to coax me on, but I was terrified of being so high up in the air. I pleaded with her to let me go back. Instead, she reminded me of what we had to look forward to on the other side.

Slowly, I took my first step onto the trestle. Then another. And another. Suddenly, my heart leapt to my throat. As the ground disappeared and the river appeared far below, I discovered that the trestle had huge gaps—gaps about a foot wide—between each board.

I cried out to my mom again, but she only urged me to go faster. "Don't look down," she said. *Don't look down?!* I thought. *If I don't look, I'm going to fall right through one of those gaps and into that raging river!* I wanted to drop to my knees and cross the bridge on all fours, but I didn't. I just kept walking, moving one board at a time. And after what seemed an eternity, I finally looked down and saw ground instead of river beneath my feet.

As quickly as I dared, I ran to safe ground and looked back on my accomplishment. When I turned around again, my family was already quite a way up the road. I ran to catch up with them, and we continued our journey to the famed oasis.

We soon picked up the path again and headed into the woods alongside the river. Just a little farther on, we pushed back the trees and peeked in. Here it was—the Garden of Eden.

The river ran gently over smooth, age-old rocks and formed a little pool before cascading down another group of rocks. The lush trees and bright-green ferns made a perfect backdrop for the most beautiful natural pool I had ever seen. The sun poked through the trees and shed a diffuse light on the garden, making the trees shine and the water glisten. It was breathtaking.

My dad went in first to test the depth of the pool and couldn't even find the bottom. Then, my brother and I dove in and swam to our hearts' content. In between the fun, we sat underneath a rock and let the water cascade over our heads. We bathed in the beauty, all of us, and felt thankful that the Lord had created it.

I don't remember crossing the train trestle on the way back, though I know I did. I remember only the beauty of that garden and what it took to get there. I was rewarded for persevering and finishing what I had set out to do.

Romans 5:3–5 says, "We also rejoice in our sufferings, because we know that suffering produces perseverance; perseverance, character; and character, hope. And hope does not disappoint us, because God has poured out his love into our hearts by the Holy Spirit, whom he has given us."

If I hadn't suffered (and yes, at the time I felt I suffered), perseverance wouldn't have been necessary. I would have lost a character-building opportunity. My hope would have been diminished. Instead, God gave me a triumphant gift, not only by helping me reach the beautiful swimming hole, but also by teaching me a valuable lesson.

In the years since then, I've faced even more severe trials. Financial challenges, the loss of a parent, cancer—these "trestles" held more dread than the bridge of my childhood. My most poignant suffering thus far came with the loss of a stillborn baby girl. The loss of my daughter forced me to choose between three paths. I could give in to desperation and try to find my own way across that river; I could turn and run in terror; or I could move forward one step at a time, believing there was something good waiting for me on the other side.

I chose to move forward. Through the prayers of many people, reading the Bible (especially the Psalms), and trusting that God had a better plan for me, I learned and grew. During that difficult trial I leaned on God's promise that out of perseverance, he would bring hope. My relationship with Jesus, which had been developing since childhood, held me up during my excruciating pain.

God poured out his love on me and helped me trust his promise of hope. And he didn't disappoint. The garden waited just ahead.

Three months after the stillbirth, I became pregnant again. Years later, as I watch my three beautiful children, I understand that God had a plan all along. I wouldn't be the person I am today without that trial. My suffering produced perseverance, character, and hope.

Now when my life's journey takes me over a treacherous trestle, I remember my Garden of Eden experience. I trust that even though the journey is sometimes slow and scary, God has the bigger picture in mind. I'm reminded that with each trial, he builds my character to be more like his; and that, at the end of the path, hope waits for me—hope poured into my heart, refreshing, like the waters in the Garden of Eden.

*Marcea Galindo is a wife, homemaker, and mother of three. When not writing or reading, she plays the violin in a string quartet, participates in her husband's real estate business, and enjoys her family.*

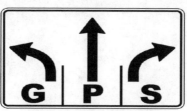

## LOST? TRY GPS
## (GOD'S POSITIONING SYSTEM)

The LORD replied, "My Presence will go with you,
and I will give you rest."
EXODUS 33:14

# OUT ON A LIMB

ANITA HIGMAN

For the most part, as a kid in the sixties, I was pretty fearless. For instance, when most girls my age got hysterical at the mention of snakes, I had one for a pet. (His name was Herby Flake, in case you were curious.) I also loved running out into the birth of a thunderstorm. The sensation felt wildly exhilarating as the fresh, cool air whipped my hair and the first signs of danger crackled all around me.

But once, my impulsiveness went too far. One afternoon, I climbed high up the mammoth old elm in our backyard.

I climbed fairly high that day, certainly high enough for me to have the beejeebies scared out of me when I finally looked down. Talk about shaking like a leaf! I clutched that elm tree with a vicious grip.

I must have screamed for my mom, because she came to my aid. My mother wasn't physically able to climb up and get me, but she stayed right at the base of the tree to talk me down.

"It'll be all right, Anita," she said. "There's a nice big limb right below you. Hold on and feel for it with your foot."

I'm sure I looked like a sloth, creeping down with such excruciating slowness. But my mom never laughed; she just loved me down that tree.

What stands out in that experience is the way I stiffened with fear and became unable to move. I clung to what I knew I had to let go of. The sky looked too close, the ground seemed like a far-away land, and all my hope had flown away with the birds.

It reminds me of the Enemy and his tactics. He's tried to convince me for years that I've sinned so many times there could be no forgiveness for the likes of me.

And my response has been a bit like that paralyzing fear that kept me glued to the tree: I froze with the worry that I may have climbed too far out on sin's branch this time. I could no longer go home. There was no turning back and no one who would want to "talk me down the tree." The Enemy had me clinging to dangerous notions I needed to let go of.

If a person could hear Satan, his snarling and vile whispers might sound like these: "How can God forgive you? You've gone too far this time. He's getting tired of hearing about the same failings. Just look how unworthy you are!"

Ever have those thoughts? You're not alone. But when we compare what Satan says about us to what the Bible says, we realize what utter nonsense we've been led to believe! Listen to Romans 3:23: "For all have sinned and fall short of the glory of God." Not certain people. *All* have sinned. And of course I'm unworthy! We *all* are.

And God reminds us in Ephesians 4:32, "Be kind and compassionate to one another, forgiving each other, just as in Christ God forgave you." In that verse, Paul told us clearly how we're to treat others, and he also revealed that Jesus forgives us when we fail. In other words, Jesus came to talk us down the old elm tree of sin. We simply need to call out to him for help. With the grace that came from the cross, we are set free from our precarious perches.

God has used the memory of my "out on a limb" experience to show me that every time I allow thoughts of my unworthiness to reign, the Enemy wins a battle (he'll never win the war, thank God!). I was saved by grace, but Satan will try to keep me paralyzed, constantly questioning if God could help me back down again.

The Lord wants us to be free and at peace. God's Word tells us how this road trip with Jesus should feel in our souls. John 14:27 reads, "Peace I leave with you; my peace I give you. I do not give to you as the world gives. Do not let your hearts be troubled and do not be afraid."

How I love that! Jesus' words are so comforting and powerful. It's an important verse to place securely in our hearts, ready to use when the Enemy attacks our peace.

So when those nasty little doubts come, and solid ground looks like a faraway land, when all hope has flown away, I will no longer hesitate to call out to Jesus. I know he'll reassure me, "It'll be all right, Anita. There's a nice big limb right below you."

And I know Jesus won't be laughing; he'll just love me down that tree.

*Award-winning author Anita Higman has sixteen books published for children and adults. Her seventeenth book, as well as a novella, will be released in 2005. For more information, visit Anita's Web site, www.anitahigman.com.*

**FAVORITE OFFBEAT ROAD TRIP EXITS**

**Avenue of the Giants, Klamath, California**—The Drive-Thru Tree can no longer be driven through, but it's still good for pictures, along with its neighbor, the Drive-On Log!

**Slide Rock State Park, Sedona, Arizona**—It's a bunch of fun sliding on your rump down the worn and slippery rocks … if you don't mind the frigid water!

# A Glimpse of Glory

KAY FLOWERS

The lightning began its flashdance of shifting brilliance, and I listened with pricked nerves as thunder rolled and curled across the river. The very air seemed alive, fairly crackling with an invisible energy. Great claps of thunder exploded, sounding depth charges over the water beyond the windows.

Like a storm, the death of my father was both sudden and unexpected. Life was abruptly thrown into a holding pattern as all five of us children boarded planes to come home for the funeral.

We comforted Mom and one another with good memories of Dad, laughing and talking far into the night. Surrounded by the walls he built, floors he laid, and windows he hung, it felt unreal that he wasn't just in the next room. The old homestead was full of flowers but empty of him.

Dad had been a steadfast rock for us. Now something very strong and solid was gone. All of a sudden, he just wasn't there anymore, and no one could fix that.

Because I was single at the time, I decided to move back home to take care of my mother, whose eyesight was fading. I left a job I loved, good friends, a lovely apartment, and a church where I finally belonged—all in two days. The rug had been yanked out from under me in more ways than one. I felt like I teetered on the edge of some vast abyss where grief mingled with an uncertain future.

Lawyers and mounds of paperwork soon overwhelmed my mother emotionally. The incessant jangling of the telephone stretched her exhausted nerves to the limit. Numerous decisions demanded her immediate attention. I helped as much as I could, but we both needed a break.

So we decided to spend a few days down at the summer cabin Dad had remodeled. He had taken a rundown cottage and crafted an impressive A-frame that perched on the upper bank of the Ohio River. In the loft, narrow windows reached to the ceiling like a rustic cathedral. At night the barges shuttled flatbeds of coal up the river, their lights rippling along the water.

At the cabin, we'd have no mail to open, no visitors to see, no decisions to make. The lapping water and songbirds would ease our sorrow and soothe our raw emotions. We could rest, remember, and heal.

During my devotional time after our arrival, I read Romans 8:18: "I consider that our present sufferings are not worth comparing with the glory that will be revealed in us." I had read that verse many times before, but this time I felt almost angered at its simplicity. What did I care for future glory, when I still hurt so deeply right now?

The promise of heavenly glory with God seemed a nebulous reward, almost a lame excuse for this painful thing called life. I knew my father reveled in the glory of heaven, and I was glad for him, but I didn't understand it all, and glory meant absolutely *nothing* to me. *Glory?* I thought. *So what?!*

Later that night, the deep rumblings of an electric storm awoke me. I went to the window to watch the storm's approach. Like an angry child, the wind picked up and tossed tree branches. The stifling air held no cooling rain.

Just then a deafening boom and blinding shaft of light blasted out the telephone line. Pure reflex jerked me away from the open window, my senses cringing. Suddenly I felt unsure and very much afraid.

I met my mother in the hallway. We stood, arms around each other, watching the strobelike display in the sky through the high windows of the loft Dad had built. As we watched, the storm grew in power, stabbing the night sky with fantastic fireworks. Some were white-hot, while some were rapid bursts of color that reverberated through the murky clouds. We watched, transfixed, for over an hour. It was terrifying, breathtaking, and in some strange way, gloriously joyful.

That's when I began to understand. This awesome, thrilling, booming, raw power that shook my very soul—this—*this* was glory! I'd seen dozens of storms before, but none had ever taught me this truth. Why had I never understood? The pulsing intensity that hurled itself in reckless, rapturous abandon across the night sky—was *glory!* Our heavenly Father engineered the marvel and then awoke us to share it with him. If earthly glory was this incredible, what must heaven be like?

I was stunned. The almighty God of the universe, my Redeemer, had this immense power in complete control. Just as my father had built a cabin strong enough to protect me from the force of the storm, my Father in heaven could protect me from the storms of life. God was right here, *now*, in an astounding revelation of majesty, standing with his children through grief and loss.

The full force of this remarkable truth made my knees weak. As I marveled in silence, my fear dissolved into praise, and my apprehension settled into deep peace.

The sky slowly trembled and faded into occasional flickers of shimmering light. The storm crossed the river, leaving in its wake downed lines and broken branches. But I somehow felt renewed, comforted, and steadied.

My mother went back to bed, but I remained wide awake, deep in thought. The God of all life had shown me a fraction of his power, the power that conquers even death. Tough decisions and deep grief could be faced with confidence now. I knew my God commanded both this present life and the afterlife as well.

The leaves torn from the trees would be replaced with fresh new leaves in the spring, and my father's buried body would be replaced with an indestructible one at the resurrection—all in good time and all under God's supreme control. My inner world now lay in perfect peace.

God had opened up his heavens to give me a glimpse of the glory that is yet to be for me; a glory that already is, for my father.

*Kay Flowers is the author of* Caleb's Daughter *(Booklocker, 2002), a Scripture-based, historical romance. She writes, gardens, and raises medicinal herbs on a farm in Ohio with her husband, Denny, and two lazy horses.*

## GOD'S GLORY DURING A HURRICANE

Does life seem like a struggle to you—a battle? Interestingly enough, most peace doesn't come until after we've fought a battle (the death of a loved one, potty training, spiritual warfare, the battle of the bulge, and storms, to name a few).

Peace might be hard to find in the midst of a Category 4 hurricane like Charley, which hit Florida the summer of 2004—while we wrote this book. I pulled out Kay Flowers' "A Glimpse of Glory," and read it to my family as the eye of the hurricane swept over our home. We found peace in knowing that God was in control … even in the middle of a hurricane! Now that's glory!

# PEACE IN THE MIDST OF STORE WARS

ELLIE KAY

As a mom of seven kids, I make lots of road trips in the car—to the school, the mall, Super Wal-Mart, and various sports practices. One day, on yet another trip to the grocery store, my five-year-old son, Joshua, and his four-year-old friend, Rachel, played with their toys in the car's backseat.

Rachel tossed her blonde curls and looked at Joshua with big, blue eyes. She smiled sweetly and said, "My daddy brought me back these Minnie Mouse dolls when he went to the state of Cal-do-forn-ya."

Rough-and-tumble Joshua replied, "Oh, yeah? Well, my papa got me these *Star Wars* toys for my birthday, and look what I can do with them!"

I heard a series of guttural noises, followed by feminine distress signals. From what I could gather, Minnie had fallen victim to a light saber.

"Joshua!" Rachel yelled as she grabbed her doll. "She doesn't wike to be poked. Wet's have a tea party instead."

By the time we arrived at the store, a doe-eyed doll had

tamed the Jedi Knight. Once inside, the children decided they wanted fried chicken from the grocery deli for lunch. Joshua wanted two whole chickens, and Rachel wanted only one leg. After a heated discussion and some cajoling, we compromised on a five-piece box of chicken for $2.99.

We sat in a booth, and the kids ate happily while I watched them. I wasn't really hungry, so I saved the two untouched pieces of chicken to eat later that afternoon.

Just a few moments into our lunch, a man who looked homeless walked into the eating area. His worn face showed years of tough living. He muttered to himself, his head twitching in small, sharp movements, and sat down across the aisle from us. He turned in his chair to stare at the three ladies eating at the table next to him. The women decided they were finished with lunch, cleared off their table, and left.

Everyone else in the deli area politely ignored the transient. My heart hurt for him, but as we gathered our things to leave, I thought, *You know, I donate lots of food to the local homeless shelter to feed guys like him.* I comforted my conscience with the idea that at least I was doing something for the man.

Then Rachel spilled her water on the floor, and I had to mop it up with napkins before we could leave. Crouching over the mess on the floor, I was only inches away from this man's battered boots. I could see their worn soles, and the weather-beaten leather revealed several holes. While in this humble position another thought came to mind: *Give him the rest of the chicken in the box.*

Before my courage melted away, I straightened up, picked up the box with one hand (my other still held wet napkins), held it out to the man, and softly asked, "Would you like some chicken?"

His dark-skinned face brightened, revealing a toothless grin as he responded enthusiastically, "Yes! Thank you very much!" He held out his hands, displaying a lack of several fingers.

I smiled and whispered, "You're welcome." The entire exchange took less than ten seconds, but the mental image of this toothless and fingerless man reaching out to receive the food remains etched in my mind.

I turned away from the man to throw away the sopping mess in my hand, and as I did so, I felt a tug at my side.

"Gee, Mama, that was a nice thing to do!" Joshua said. Then he ran off with Rachel to get free cookies at the bakery counter.

As we drove out of the store's parking lot, the backseat *Star Wars*/Minnie Mouse conflict started up again. But in the midst of the war between the toys, I felt peaceful as a still, small voice spoke to my heart: *When you've done it to the least of these, Ellie, you've done it to me.*

*Ellie Kay is a best-selling author of seven books and is trade-marked as "America's Family Financial Expert." She is a frequent guest on CNBC's* Power Lunch *and* Money Matters. *She and her husband, Bob, have seven children and live in Palmdale, California.*

## STARSHINE'S HOW'S YOUR INNERSTATE?

### Questions for Reflection and Journaling

- Have you heard a still, small voice asking you to help someone in need? What was your response?
- How does God speak to you?
- Do your children see you assisting others? If not, how could you alter your lifestyle to make that type of ministry happen?
- Which do you prefer: white or dark chicken meat?

# OXYGEN

CHRIS KARCHER

Was I crazy? Should I walk away from a lucrative career—a career I'd had for twenty years, a career that included such tasks as managing multimillion-dollar projects—"just" to write a book? Should I pack in the paycheck and trust my savings account would carry me as I pursued my dream? After all, living my passion was a noble thought, but I also liked to eat!

In the middle of the night, up fretting and debating, I searched the Bible for answers to my dilemma. And as I read, I suddenly remembered a long-ago summer rafting trip....

The river was running high. My husband, Dave, and I floated with a group of friends in the most treacherous stretch of white water in the Snake River outside of Jackson Hole, Wyoming. Professional photographers regularly climbed down the precipitous mountain slope to the water's edge and snapped photos of the rafters. They hoped those same rafters would survive the white water and purchase their photos at the end of the trip.

I had chosen my raft carefully, and it was BIG. The oarsman, a good friend of mine, rafted professionally and had never flipped a boat.

We entered the rapids with momentum and hit the waves head-on. To survive, all we passengers had to do was hold on; surely, the raft would not flip end over end.

The rubber roller coaster journeyed up and down over the swells. I wedged my toes between the tube and the floor of the raft to anchor myself for the jarring ride. As rapids crashed above my head, my hands seized the aluminum tube on top of the raft. Waves engulfed the boat, and I tightened my grip.

Up and up we went. My fingernails dug into the palms of my hands until we were up, up, and ... over. Thunderous waves had flipped our raft end over end, even though we knocked into them squarely and with plenty of speed.

All six of us were thrown beneath the raft and trapped underwater in the churning, forty-three-degree white water. Whether you can swim or not makes little difference at that point. You go where the river torrents hurl you.

The flailing arms and legs of the other rafters struck me as we struggled underneath the raft. Oddly, I found those flailing arms and legs comforting because it meant I was not alone.

We should have left the raft. The safest action would have been for us to let go of the railing along the top of the raft as it flipped. But my fellow rafters and I feared leaving the comfort and security of our raft so much that before we knew it, we found ourselves trapped underwater.

I thrashed about in the water beneath the raft. Needing air, I pushed upward but crashed into the rubber ceiling. The white water spun me back down. I wrestled again toward the surface.

And once again, the raft acted as a barricade between the sky and me. I wished I had filled my lungs with air before landing in the water.

I tussled. The water churned. Finally, I popped out from underneath the raft and gulped in air. Oxygen! I could breathe again.

Several months later, in the early hours of the morning, I asked myself, *Is my job now my raft? Am I clinging to it as the waves crash upon my head? Perhaps I'm opting to stay employed because it pays well. Am I afraid to leave the security of my comfort zone?*

And with that question, I got my answer: the fear of leaving my comfort zone was keeping me from living my dream. Venturing away from the raft is risky.

And I realized, finally, that finding my calling—writing— was like breathing. I simply had to do it. So I left my job to write a book, *Relationships of Grace.*

People have commented about how disciplined I must be to write a book. True, writing requires commitment, but love motivates me more than discipline. The book lived inside of me. It's been a joy letting it out. Why wouldn't I want to do something I love?

Discovering my passion required that I risk leaving the security of my comfort zone. If I'd not chosen to leave a lucrative twenty-year career in computer software engineering, my dream would still be burning within me.

Since my journey down the rapids, I've learned the only *real* security I have is in God. Remember how the flailing arms and legs of the other people underneath the raft reassured me because they meant I was not alone? If people trapped under a raft, struggling for air, calmed me, imagine my comfort level if

I would only remember that God, the Supreme Comforter, is with me always.

The Proverb teaches us to "Trust in the *Lord* with all thine heart; and lean not unto thine own understanding. In all thy ways acknowledge him, and he shall direct thy paths" (Prov. 3:5–6 KJV). By surrendering to and trusting in God, I received the courage to live in accordance with God's plan for my life—regardless of how scary that plan seemed.

The line between work and play is blurred now. Because I love it, my "job" does not feel like work. It's fun; so much so that at the end of the week, I sometimes even feel a twinge of sorrow because the workweek is over.

God has given me the grace—the oxygen—I need to trust his plans. And I have been richly rewarded.

*Chris Karcher teaches people how to live with meaning through grace. She is a speaker and author of* Relationships of Grace *(Faithworks, 2003), a companion workbook, and* Amazing Things I Know About You *(Faithworks, 2003). Both are available at www.relationshipsofgrace.com.*

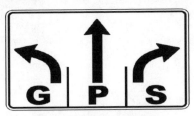

## LOST? TRY GPS
## (GOD'S POSITIONING SYSTEM)

"For I know the plans I have for you,"
says the LORD.
"They are plans for good and not for disaster,
to give you a future and a hope."
JEREMIAH 29:11 NLT

# PARDON ME

GINGER PLOWMAN

Walking into the crowded police station, children in tow, I held my head down in hopes that no one would recognize me. After all, as the owner of a restaurant known for serving the love of Jesus along with its fried chicken, I should have known better than to exceed the speed limit by twenty-two miles per hour.

Shame pricked my heart as the Bible verses displayed on our restaurant walls and parking lot marquee flashed in my head. My mad dash home from the grocery store had tarnished my testimony. Now it was time to pay the piper.

Hoping to zip in, pay my dues, and zip back out again unnoticed, I approached the receptionist and handed her the evidence of my dirty deed. In my quietest voice, I said, "Yes ... um ... I would like to pay for this speeding ticket."

The woman behind the desk, whom I'll call "Betty," was obviously hard of hearing. Her response could not have been any louder if it were amplified through a stadium megaphone: "I'm sorry, ma'am, but you'll have to speak up. Did you say that you needed to pay for a speeding ticket?"

My face reddened as heads turned to behold the dangerous criminal. I thought how nice it would be if my pastor suddenly glided in and rescued me with his "I want every head bowed and every eye closed" line, but it didn't happen.

Just when I thought it couldn't get any worse, Betty began to read off the details of my offense. "Mm, mm, mm, child—fifty-seven in a thirty-five. You sure know how to put the pedal to the metal, don't you? What were you thinking?"

I could feel the disapproval of the audience as they glanced from me to my children, the innocent victims of the could-have-been-fatal accident.

"I told her to slow down," announced my youngest child.

*Great. Just great.*

Betty shook her head in disgust and began typing in my information. But then her fingers stilled suddenly. "Wait a minute," she said. "Is this your work number?"

"Yes," I mumbled. There on the sheet was the phone number to our restaurant, Jim Bob's Chicken Fingers. Apparently, Betty had called in an order or two, because she recognized the number.

"I know you!" she gasped. "You're Mrs. Jim Bob!"

My status (in her eyes) rose immediately—from "America's Most Wanted" to her most treasured friend. She began to celebrate my presence by announcing exactly who I was to everyone in the lobby.

I realized that passing out cold would frighten my children, so I simply smiled and endured the scene my new friend was creating. Trying to put an end to the nightmare, I attempted to get her back to the task at hand. "How much do I owe you?" I asked.

Nice try, but no dice.

Betty grinned from ear to ear. "Why, we can't have Mrs. Jim Bob paying for a speeding ticket!" she said. "Let me see what I can do."

While her intentions were kind, I could have crawled under a rock and died from embarrassment. Once again, I tried to take care of the debt so that I could hightail it out of there. "Oh, no, that's okay," I pleaded. "I was speeding and I should pay for the ticket." But Betty would have none of it.

After summoning half of the police force to her desk, she explained to the uniformed law enforcers that it was a mortal sin to issue "Mrs. Jim Bob" a traffic citation. Amazingly, they all agreed to drop the charges.

I guess all of those free leftover chicken fingers delivered to the station had finally paid off! I felt like some sort of hero as they patted my back and expressed gratitude for all of their gratis, late-night snacks. The only thing missing was a big "hip, hip, hooray!" and a ride on their shoulders. Funny how things work out.

On the ride home, I reflected on the significance of the situation. I'd been let off the hook simply because I acknowledged the police officers by serving them free food. It didn't seem fair. A few pieces of chicken (that would have been thrown out anyway) hardly seemed worth the pardon they offered. It just didn't feel right. I considered whipping my car around, racing (within the speed limit, of course) back to the station, and insisting that I pay my debt.

But then I remembered another debt—a much greater debt—that I had owed. A debt that was paid in full by the blood of Jesus Christ. "For Christ also suffered once for sins, the just for the unjust, that He might bring us to God" (1 Peter 3:18 NKJV).

It doesn't seem fair that Jesus would pay for my sins. I did nothing to deserve his pardon. Yet, he paid my debt. He offered a pardon. The stakes to free me from debt were high—in fact, they cost Jesus his very life.

I was pardoned from my sin and let off the hook from the penalty simply because I accepted his offer, acknowledging Jesus as my Lord and Savior and asking his forgiveness. To reject his payment and insist on paying it myself would be a slap in his face. I am eternally grateful that Jesus Christ paid the exorbitant price in order to cancel my debt.

I think I'll let Betty and all my friends at the police department pardon my debt there, too! Why not?

*Ginger Plowman, author of* Don't Make Me Count to Three! *(Shepherd Press, 2004), is the founder of Preparing the Way Ministries, through which she speaks at women's events and parenting conferences across the country. Visit her Web site at www.gingerplowman.com.*

**FAVORITE OFFBEAT ROAD TRIP EXITS**

**Gatorland, Orlando, Florida**—Disney, look out ... it's time for the Gator Jumparoo show, where full, raw, and (thankfully) dead chickens are fed to jumping alligators. Children, do not attempt this at home!

**Weeki Wachee Springs, Florida**—You have to wonder if Ariel swam her way from Weeki Wachee to Disney World after you watch real "live" mermaids perform aquabatics and musical numbers including a tribute to America!

# MOMS FINDING OUR SPIRITUAL GROOVE

JANE JARRELL AND RACHEL ST. JOHN-GILBERT

There's something about motherhood that tends to catapult a woman into a journey toward true spirituality. Often, the search is driven by theological questions uttered forth from the peanut-buttered mouths of babes: "Where did my fish go when he died?" and "How do you know for sure there's a heaven?" We long for our children to have the peace that only God can give in this crazy world. We want our kids in church, even if we ourselves are spiritual lightweights whose thoughts turn to candy instead of deity when we hear the word "divinity."

If we were church girls most of our lives, parenthood may cause us to long for a more authentic, intimate connection with Christ. Or possibly we need to wrestle with our faith in Christianity altogether for a period of time before embracing it wholeheartedly again.

Regardless of where you are in your spiritual life, the fact remains that most mothers begin to feel the heat when little ones come along. Precious souls are looking to us for direction. It's as if each child is holding out an empty cup, and we desperately want to fill it with something real, true, and everlasting. The jig is up—and, pardon the pun—we moms have to deliver.

## Rachel's Journey—From Gray to Grace

I had been a churchgoing gal my entire life, and the faith of my childhood held pretty steady through college and early marriage. It wasn't until my firstborn turned three that I sensed a gap in my relationship with God. What I *truly* felt often conflicted with what I knew I *should* feel. I wanted to have good thoughts, kind words, and appropriate feelings, but that was often not the case. I knew the pat answers to life and godliness, but I couldn't seem to whip myself into shape.

So I found myself in an "inventory" mode—and I didn't like most of what I saw. At times, I would let my temper flare more quickly and hotly than I thought possible. To make matters worse, in moments of acute distress, naughty words often popped into my brain. This "good girl" was mortified! "What must God think of me *now?*" I would moan to myself, slinking into a pit of self-condemnation.

One morning, overwhelmed with the tough questions of life and with (what I felt was) my mediocre existence, I sat down with a journal and a cup of coffee. As my eyes brimmed with tears, I uttered softly, "Dear God, show me what's going on inside of me." At that moment, I put pen to paper—for two hours straight.

When I finished, I had detailed pivotal memories and thoughts from my life. Some were pain-tinged memories of an overly sensitive younger me trying to find my place in this world. Other entries listed hopes and dreams that I had locked away and was afraid to dust off, for fear they wouldn't come true. And possibly the most significant revelation was that there had been a veil covering my existence for a long time—a veil of condemnation.

In those moments, I felt as if God were saying, "Stop condemning yourself. You have to be completely open and honest with me—and whether your feelings and thoughts are right or wrong, you have to trust me with them." I could literally visualize God saying, "Come here," with a smile of acceptance and wide-open arms.

Shortly after that experience, my "do-over" process began. I read books like *Sometimes I Feel Like Running Away from Home* and the classic *Codependent No More*. I sought out a mentor with whom I could be completely, soul-shakingly honest. I read books about how to deal with the frustrations of childrearing. My pre-midlife crisis was a crazy, scary, wonderful time—and a time of much-needed growth.

My quest for a closer connection with God began because I wanted more out of life, relationships, and spirituality. I wanted to truly feel the freedom of grace personified through Jesus Christ. I wanted to be a godly mom for my kids. And, praise God, he slowly began freeing me. I still lose my temper with my children sometimes, and yes, I still have "bad" thoughts (don't we all?), but now I know that God still loves me. And he loves my children even more than I do—so I don't have to be perfect!

I experienced an epiphany. I came to the realization that God is more interested in my love than in whether or not my behavior is flawless. You can't experience true love and intimacy without knowing the darker side of a person and loving him or her in spite of it—or through it. I came to believe that God wanted all of me—both the good and the bad.

Every mother must take a spiritual journey with her Creator. Because of my journey, I rarely feel the sting of condemnation anymore. I no longer walk around with a gray cloud covering me because God has made me right with him. He did so by dying for my sins—those I do willingly and those I do unwittingly. It's truly amazing ... amazing grace.

## JANE'S JOURNEY—FROM HERE TO ETERNITY

"Grace so amazing and love so divine makes life worth living and brings joy sublime." I, too, was conceived in the church, so to speak. I grew up under the guidance of a minister father and a seminary-educated mother. It was as normal as breathing to say a prayer before a meal, discuss the preacher's sermon, or ask God for guidance on a variety of issues.

But as an adult outside of the family fold, I grappled with my identity. I wondered, *Does my worldview edge closer to the religious right or the liberal left?* I often felt like a hybrid of Jerry Falwell and Ted Kennedy. And after I became a mother and realized another little life was totally dependent upon me, I wondered if I was strong enough spiritually and emotionally to direct and mold another soul.

However, nothing stopped me in my spiritual tracks quite like my daughter's salvation experience. With the innocence of a child's heart, our seven-year-old invited Jesus to be Lord of her life. It was somewhat surreal. For months she had been incessantly asking questions—the kind of questions that stump stalwart theologians. When Sarah finally said, "Well, I believe that Jesus died for me, and I want to go to heaven," my husband asked her if she was ready to ask Jesus into her heart. She expressed quite succinctly that she knew what she was doing.

The three of us sat together on the couch, and Mark read through the *Four Spiritual Laws* tract, attempting to make sure Sarah understood to the best of her ability what she was doing.

We knew the questions without the tract, but this was a highly emotional time. We didn't want to put words in Sarah's mouth, and we wanted her to feel secure in her decision. Soon it was clear she "got it." Her capacity to understand amazed me. What childlike faith and honest abandon! So Mark began the prayer, Sarah prayed with him, and I cried. We stood on holy ground right in the middle of our den.

At bedtime that night, Sarah told me she could feel Jesus in her heart. I asked her how that felt, and she said her heart felt "soft." What a perfect analogy. I prayed for her earnestly that night, "Lord, give her sweet abundant joy, give her peace that only you can provide, and help her to truly and consistently live as one walking with you."

As I watched my child choose Christ, joy filled my heart. But at the same time, the responsibility of it all came crashing in. Again, questions filled me: *Will I disciple her correctly? What if I "lose it" with Sarah—how will I explain that Christian mommies still make mistakes sometimes? What should the next step be? Do I get her a Bible with her name embossed on it? Do I put her in line for early enrollment at Moody Bible Institute?*

My spiritual life ebbs and flows—more ebbing than flowing at times. My intentions are often stellar, but good intentions alone would not pave the path to a righteous life for my child. I don't want to let my daughter down. I want to keep the beauty and innocence of embracing Christ, but I still have the hard task of daily living and a sinful nature to battle. It is difficult to hold on to the "softness" of our early conversion experience and feelings of near-euphoria (both for the parent and the child). I felt the weight of responsibility. Frankly, when I looked in the spiritual mirror I saw Don Knotts instead of Arnold Schwarzenegger.

In the end, it caused me to take inventory. I, too, made the decision to give my heart to Christ as a young child, but was I living this decision each day? No. In fact, I have let the "mundane" steal my joy. I am often so focused on "things to do" that joy has to elbow its way into my day planner. Yikes!

We have but one purpose in life: to glorify God. I frequently stray far from that as I try to be the epitome of June Cleaver.

Isn't it astonishing to see the intertwining of our spiritual lives with those we love? All these thoughts came rushing through my mind just as my child made the most significant decision of her life. It proved to be a pivotal moment in my spiritual journey.

After praying about my questions, I realized that the first area of my spiritual life that I let slide is Bible study. My family and I attend church each Sunday. Our pastor and Sunday school teacher give great messages. But I'm not always personally consistent to stay in the Word and have it permeate my being.

Elizabeth George shared the following in her book *A Woman after God's Own Heart* (Harvest House, 1997): "There are three stages in Bible reading: Cod-liver-oil stage when you take it like a medicine; Shredded-wheat stage when it's nourishing but dry; and Peaches and cream stage when it's consumed with passion and pleasure."

Rachel and I pray that you'll join us on our journey. As we travel the road from condemnation to grace, we're asking God to grant us the discipline and the passion to integrate his Word, his truth, and his direction into our lives. And we're asking for peaches and cream!

*Rachel St. John-Gilbert is the author of* Wake Up Laughing— Offbeat Devotions for the Unconventional Woman *(Barbour,*

*2004). She lives in Texas with her husband and three children.*

*Jane Jarrell (www.janejarrell.net) is the author of twelve books and coauthor of twenty. Her newest book is* Secrets of a Midlife Mom *(NavPress, 2004). She and her husband, Mark, have one daughter and live in Texas.*

## STARSHINE'S SMILE MARKERS

### Twenty Great Things about Leaving My Twenties

1. Understanding all the inside jokes on kids' cartoons.
2. Owning a home.
3. Realizing my parents are pretty smart, after all!
4. Giving surprise parties.
5. Paying off those pesky student loans.
6. Making good memories.
7. Deepening friendships.
8. Attending high school reunions.
9. Having lunch with friends.
10. Staying up as late as I want (or can!).
11. Seeing my friends have kids.
12. Knowing the beliefs I have are mine and not just my parents'.
13. Discovering that everything old is new again (just wish I could fit into those pants from high school).
14. Having more confidence in my abilities.
15. Experiencing less stress about the things I can't do well.
16. Finding faith that grows deeper.
17. Realizing hope that lasts longer.
18. Experiencing love that grows stronger.
19. Discovering forgiveness that grows wider.
20. Being alive to enjoy it all!

# HIPPIES IN HEAVEN

NANCY C. ANDERSON

I was a good girl from a wholesome Minnesota family. We went to a traditional mainline church every Sunday and always said appropriate prayers at our properly set dinner table. I had a strong commitment to my Sunday school class and an undying devotion to the "Religious Ringers" handbell choir. And I assumed that all of my good behavior would get me into heaven.

Then, in 1972, a singing group called The Jesus People came to Winona Senior High School to perform at an after-school assembly. (Yes, in the "olden days," Christians were allowed into the public schools!) I was full of self-righteous thoughts as I walked into the auditorium, wondering what hippies with long hair, bare feet, and ragged bell-bottoms could possibly teach someone like me about God. I even questioned whether hippies would be allowed into heaven. Probably not!

But as I listened to their folk songs and stories, I noticed they had something I didn't: peace. I knew all *about* Jesus, but they knew Jesus personally. I memorized Bible verses to win gold ribbons, but they stored away verses to win souls.

I started to cry as they sang a song called "I Wish We'd All Been Ready" by Larry Norman. The song is based on Luke 17:34, which says that some people will be left behind when Jesus takes his true followers to heaven. I knew I wasn't "ready" and realized that I'd be one of those left behind.

The group's leader saw me crying and said, "If you'd like to know how you can have Jesus as your personal Lord, Savior, and friend, please raise your hand."

I lifted my arm as if it were spring-loaded. I noticed some of the other kids pointing and laughing at me, but I just thought, *Why aren't they raising their hands? Don't they know how important this is?*

Then one of the singers took the microphone, looked directly at me, and asked, "Would you be willing to take a public stand for Jesus?"

I nodded, and, through my tears, said, "Yes."

She continued. "Will you get out of your seat, come down here, and pray with my friends?" She pointed to a group of college-age women by the side of the stage.

Before I knew what was happening, I was down in front, hugging one of them and asking her to pray. "Hurry," I said. "Jesus is waiting for me."

She introduced me to Jesus—not the historical figure, but the real, living person. When I asked him to be my Savior, he made me a new creation. I saw with new eyes, heard with new ears, and spoke with a new mouth as I said, "Oh, Jesus, thank you for making me whole."

My makeover, my transformation, took less than a minute. As I spoke the request, he forgave my sins. As I opened the door, he entered my heart. I began a new life—full of abundance and peace.

And I knew, without a doubt, I would not be left behind.

*Nancy C. Anderson (www.NCAwrites.com) is a speaker and the author of* The "Greener Grass" Syndrome: Growing Affair-Proof Hedges Around Your Marriage *(Kregel, 2005). Nancy lives in Southern California with her husband and their teenage son.*

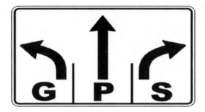

## LOST? TRY GPS
## (GOD'S POSITIONING SYSTEM)

Therefore, since we have been justified through faith, we have peace with God through our Lord Jesus Christ.

ROMANS 5:1

# GUARDED WARDROBES

SUE CHAPMAN BROWN

Have you ever thought about what your luggage goes through when you turn it over to the airline employees? Most of the time, we're so relieved not to carry it anymore that we don't worry about handing it over. We watch the uniformed men and women weigh our bags, attach the luggage stickers, and plop them on the conveyor belt.

We're pretty trusting. For all we know, there's a Samsonite gorilla waiting behind those rubber flaps—or maybe our luggage has to maneuver through some kind of obstacle course, complete with sharp crags and burning coals, before it reaches the airplane.

Nowadays, we are not even allowed to lock our bags. Yet we willingly submit them, knowing they'll be opened, searched, and abused as the workers attempt to shove all those expanded, fluffed-out items back into our suitcase.

Several years ago, on the night before a trip to Philadelphia, I laid out outfits for the thirteen meetings I would attend during a two-week speaking tour. My husband laughed when I asked if he thought seven suits were too many to take.

"No," he said. "Take them all. Knowing you, some will be too hot and some too cold, some will end up with lipstick or tears on the shoulders, and some you'll decide 'just don't look right!' Take them all!"

So I did. I packed seven suits with matching shoes, tops, and jewelry—enough to make plenty of outfits. I handed over my heavy suitcases at the Dallas terminal with relief. Gorillas never crossed my mind.

The flight into Philadelphia was quick and comfortable. Just three and a half hours after my departure, I stood in the baggage claim area, chatting and catching up with the two pastors' wives hosting my trip.

One of the women, Irene, is a trip herself, and she kept our little group in stitches as we waited. We were so busy laughing that it surprised us to realize we were the only ones still standing there, and that only one of my suitcases had come through. The same thought dawned on all three of us at once: *lost luggage!*

But just as I turned to go to the window and report the absence of my garment bag, my mouth dropped open in complete shock. Staring at the conveyor belt, I shrieked in disbelief, "That's mine!"

All six eyes in our little group focused on a horrific sight. What we saw, circling around toward us, was the left sleeve to my brand-new, taupe, beaded suit.

As I bent over, trembling, to claim my sleeve, Irene sprang to the payphone to call her husband. Unbelievably, the conveyor belt continued to spit out the contents of my shredded garment bag (all seven suits!), one scattered piece at a time. Some of the recovered items were as big as a skirt, but some were as small as a lapel. Two jackets (or partial jackets) were melted together.

Someone gave me a dilapidated cardboard box to carry my goods home, and the airline promised to replace the bag. However, while she was on the phone, Irene repeated out loud her husband's question: "Is Sue being assertive?" As she took his directions, her eyes danced to suppress her laughter. Pastor Dave knew I struggled in that area.

He told us—emphatically—not to leave the airport without getting some answers. His words filled us with determination.

Arms linked together, we marched through the airport like sisters on a mission.

At our insistence, the airline, which will not be named, assigned some workers to take us into the back room and set up a special table. We laid all the pieces of my destroyed clothing down, and they took pictures.

One whole skirt had just the hemline disfigured. I thought I might be able to fix it, so I picked it up to take home. One of the officers took it from me and tossed it in the trash. "You either claim the whole bag as lost, or none of it," she snapped.

Were gorillas to blame? I can't be sure. The airline said that my bag had been caught in some part of the conveyer belt. Before the day ended, I was thanking the Lord for pastors and their God-given authority. Pastor Dave walked us through the entire situation via telephone. He taught us "Assertiveness 101," as we later called it, and guided us as we made demands and requirements of the airline. We left with a check in hand. It didn't cover complete replacement or solve the immediate problem, but it was a check nevertheless!

As we pulled away from the airport, I pondered the events of the day and recognized several blessings. There had been no tears. The force of godly sisterhood had tramped victoriously around that airport with our little cardboard box full of evidence.

We had drawn from the wells of grace as my weak knees were strengthened and my hands held high. We had laughed at the situation as we persevered with peace!

We stopped at a resale store to find an outfit for the next day, and then at the house of one of Irene's friends, who just happened to be my size. She lent me a few outfits. Again, God provided! Finally, tired and hungry yet grateful, we decided to eat at the only local diner still open. As we bowed to give thanks for our late dinner, the Lord reminded me of the text for my first message: "Behold, I come like a thief! Blessed is he who stays awake and keeps his clothes with him, so that he may not go naked and be shamefully exposed" (Rev. 16:15). I couldn't help giggling—even with my head bowed and my eyes closed.

To prepare for my teaching, I had studied the armor of God and the garments of righteousness we've been given as Christians. The verse from Revelation clearly implied the importance of guarding those garments by wearing them.

Before my ordeal, this passage had made me picture a woman standing spread-eagled across the doors of her closet, trying to guard her clothes from any intruder. I was all set to share that picture with my audience and explain that to guard our garments, we must be seen wearing them.

Ah ... but God! He had now added another angle to his message, showing me that we guard our spiritual clothes by keeping them with us at all times—and that once we've been entrusted with that job, it's up to us and no one else. Also, we are not to be passive in our guarding. If we are, our garments—so necessary in this evil world—might end up in shreds.

Since that adventure, I think of the vivid lesson God taught me each and every time I hand my luggage to the stranger at the counter in the airport.

*Susan Chapman Brown is founder and president of Arising to Excellence Ministries. An ordained minister, she serves the body of Christ as an international speaker and inspirational writer. She resides in Grapevine, Texas.*

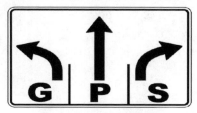

## LOST? TRY GPS
## (GOD'S POSITIONING SYSTEM)

She is clothed with strength and dignity;
she can laugh at the days to come.
PROVERBS 31:25

## STARSHINE'S SMILE MARKERS

The better you become acquainted
with God, the less tensions you feel
and the more peace you possess.

CHARLES L. ALLEN,

*ALL THINGS ARE POSSIBLE THROUGH PRAYER*

# THE GROOVY GRASSHOPPER

EVA MARIE EVERSON

I spotted the grasshopper on an outside window ledge. Throughout the morning I watched him basking in the warm sunshine, his wings periodically quivering in the gentle breeze.

Near noon, as the January wind increased, the grasshopper stirred from his resting place. He inched his way up the tempered glass, and I noticed that one of his back legs was missing.

His antennae worked furiously, guiding him. Inch by inch, push by push, with only five legs and the wind force against him, he finally reached his goal. A while later, satisfied with his victory, he returned to the ledge.

His journey reminded me of a time back in 1993, when we'd moved to Florida to take advantage of a business opportunity for my husband. At the time of the move, we considered it a most wonderful gift from God.

Eight months later, though, it seemed a curse from the Enemy as my husband and I stared at a letter informing us that we had placed our faith in a farce. In a moment that is difficult to describe, our lives—and our social position—changed forever.

We went from having the world by the tail to having everything we'd worked for slip through our fingers.

In all honesty, I don't think we truly realized the full impact of the situation. Within months, our savings vanished. We were forced to cash in our life insurance policies and IRAs, sell many of our possessions, and move into a small, two-bedroom apartment with a fraction of the space we'd had a year earlier. We even filed for bankruptcy—a moment I'll never forget. Who knew one had to *have* money to stand before a judge and claim to not have any at all? And finally, in our darkest hour, we requested governmental assistance in the form of welfare and food stamps.

The hours stretched into days and weeks of unending listlessness, like on hot, humid summer afternoons when you're keenly aware of every breath that you take.

Though today I ask God to keep me from ever going through the experience again, incredible miracles took place during this difficult time of my life.

My husband and I had always been the "givers." I'm not speaking just in terms of tithing, but in giving to the needy. Previously, I'd assumed that receiving a gift was easy. It's not. It is uncomfortably humbling. Many days I prayed on the walk to our mailbox, asking God how we were going to pay the rent or the electric bill. I'd nearly collapse to my knees when I'd find an unexpected check, given to help us meet our needs.

Many times I stood before the open refrigerator, staring into its white barrenness and praying, "Lord, exactly what are you planning for dinner tonight?" Often, before I could close the refrigerator door, the phone would ring, and I'd answer, only to hear, "Just wanted to see if you were free for dinner tonight. We're buying." It happened time and again.

One afternoon, a friend called and asked if she could come over. I sensed by the tone of her voice that she had an agenda.

"Certainly," I answered.

When she arrived, we sat on the sofa, side by side, while she shared with me that she'd recently been blessed financially. "I wanted to share part of it with you," she continued, slipping a sealed envelope toward me. Amid all those countless miracles, one stands above the rest: the miracle that took place inside my heart. Never had I clung to the Word of God as I did during that trial. Never had I felt his comforting hand on my shoulder as I felt it then. His wisdom grew in my heart, forming me into what he had always desired for me.

During this period, I participated in a "la-di-da" charity fashion show. One afternoon, I stepped into a killer outfit, let the hair dresser fuss over me and the makeup artist frou-frou me, and pranced down the catwalk in front of the rich and fabulous, dripping in jewelry that could have easily paid that month's rent.

I had to chuckle. *Come Monday morning,* I thought, *I'll be standing in a food stamp line wearing old jeans and a T-shirt. But, sister, don't I look marvelous right now?*

After the fashion show, the owner of the boutique approached me. "Eva Marie, if you like any of the clothes or jewelry you wore today, you can buy it at 20 percent off. By the way, the second outfit you modeled looked like a million bucks on you."

It may as well have *cost* a million bucks. I couldn't afford it or any of the outfits I'd modeled even if she'd offered an 80 percent discount. But, oh, how I wanted that second outfit! It had my name written all over it! A year earlier, I'd have bought it and thought nothing of it. But at this point, I didn't have money to shop at a thrift store, much less an upscale boutique.

Shortly after, on a brisk winter morning came my defining moment. As I passed out of a public building and made my way toward the old jalopy I now drove, I saw my husband's ex-business partner's wife wearing ... you guessed it ... my outfit. I cried all the way home and begged God to explain this to me.

"Isn't it enough that I'm down on my knees? Does life have to kick me in the gut, too?" I asked through my tears.

I nearly ran into our apartment and bolted the door behind me. As I did so, the phone rang. It was my dear, dear friend Donald. "Listen," he began, "I don't know why ... but God impressed on me that I need to tell you this: It doesn't matter what you drive, where you live, how much money you have, or what clothes you wear. What matters is that you trust him."

This was more than just a nugget of truth at the appropriate time. It was God's precious way of telling me life would return to normal one day, even though my definition of "normal" would most certainly change. From that moment, wounded and battered like that five-legged grasshopper, I turned my faith upward and began to inch down the road toward peace and perfection.

Now, more than a decade later, I've decided I won't achieve perfection in this lifetime. But I've also decided that peace comes with faith and learning to trust God completely. He's restored everything back to us—and more.

Recently, my husband sold the business he rebuilt from scratch (and a whole lot of faith) after an injury made it necessary for him to rest for an undetermined period of time. After he signed all the dotted lines and was once again jobless, my first thought was, *God? Are we on this road again?*

And then I laughed. Yeah, maybe so. Then again, maybe not. Either way, God is totally in control, and I'm just going to ride shotgun and see what happens.

I guess that's peace.

Groovy.

*Eva Marie Everson is a Groovy Chick who has written, cowritten, or ghosted nearly fifteen books and other fun works. She is a contributing author to various magazines and a featured writer for www.Crosswalk.com.*

## THE IWANNA, INEEDA, IGOTTA HAVE SISTERS: PEACE IN THE MIDST OF MATERIALISM

I'm not an especially materialistic person, but every spring, when Target comes out with the coolest new camping gear, I get a little "needy."

One weekend, my brood packed up and went camping with two other families. As we drove the campground's dirt roads, we checked out the array of tents, pop-ups, chairs, and clotheslines. And after we arrived at our sites, we three wives began to compare notes: "What is the deal with those foldable chairs with drink holders and foot rests?" and "Did you see that pop-up you can stand in? … the one with air conditioning? I bet it even has a bathroom!" and "How 'bout that forest green tent with three wings, complete with stargazing roof?"

We were quite a trio, envying the newfangled gadgets everyone else had, while bemoaning our garage-sale-purchased gear. When we finally realized what we sounded like, we christened ourselves "The Iwanna, Ineeda, and Igotta Have Sisters."

Here we were in God's "great outdoors," minutes from the magnificent Atlantic Ocean, and our thoughts were on someone else's campfire chicken roaster!

Simple comparisons can steal the peace God wants us to have. Perhaps you've struggled with the "Iwanna, Ineeda, Igotta Have" syndrome yourself. Maybe you always expected that when you reached your forties, you'd be in a better home. Or you want a pool for your kids and their friends. Has life thrown a curveball and your finances haven't turned out as you expected? You reason that you deserve stuff because you've worked hard. And then you join the Have family: "Iwanna," "Ineeda," and "Igotta."

Here are the Haves' top three killers of contentment:

1. Comparison
2. Comparison!
3. Comparison!!

But what's the cure? Listen to this verse: "I have learned to be content in whatever circumstances I am" (Phil. 4:11 NASB). Okay, most of us have heard that verse before, but did you know Paul wrote that Scripture while in prison? Yes, he was at *peace* in *prison!*

Have you ever wailed, "Why can't I be like that?" We want to be a peaceful waif, floating through life, without a concern or expectation in the world. But how do we get rid of these awful feelings of envy and discontent?

Actually, I've asked myself that question quite often. But I've discovered one thing that helps me. When desperate enough, I give in and totally focus on Jesus. (Why do I wait until I'm desperate?) But the more I focus on and truly worship Jesus, the more I take my eyes off *moi.* Here are some practical ways I get my eyes off myself: read the Bible, sing praise songs, enjoy nature, or talk and listen to Jesus. For more ideas on how to worship the way God made you, a great read is *Sacred Pathways* (Zondervan, 2002) by Gary Thomas.

And now I think I'll go camp in the Word. Wanna come?

# THE HORSE STOOD STILL

LILLY ALLISON

I've learned a lot from horses over the years. I've learned they sometimes gallop off a trail and stop suddenly for a drink at their favorite watering hole, sending the unsuspecting rider into an icy-cold stream. I've discovered horses have an inner ability to judge people, and that if a horse steps on your foot, bones may break. But the most important lesson I've ever learned from a horse happened at our church's family camp one summer in Colorado.

Every day the camp offered trail rides, and every day I successfully avoided going anywhere near the stables, because I knew people would ask if I wanted to go along. Riding a horse was the last thing I wanted to do at camp. My history with horses was not pleasant.

But one day my husband, Don, decided we should go for a trail ride. He assured me it would be fine. The guide, Linda, promised she would give me a slow-moving horse and said she would stay by me. One of my best friends was going too, and she convinced me it would be fun. I must have been oxygen-deprived in the mountain air because I agreed to go.

Linda brought me a massive horse named Dusty, who didn't look so good. I thought about asking for another animal because I wasn't too sure this one would make it by herself, much less with a rider. But Linda said Dusty was a trail horse and would make it just fine. After Linda told me how to mount the horse, I somehow got in the saddle. We toured the hills, dales, and abandoned mine sites, and I actually started to relax and enjoy the ride. Dusty was a great horse. I'd reach over and pet her, and she'd look back. I really liked her.

When we got back to the stables, Linda told me how to get off the horse and said she'd be back in a few minutes to get Dusty. Then she went to take care of the other horses. As I started to dismount, my pant leg got stuck under the saddle, so I leaned forward to pull the material out. Then I confidently swung my leg over the saddle and expected to slide down. But apparently, when I leaned forward to untangle my pant leg, I hooked the saddle horn with my bra, so I wasn't going anywhere.

Everyone else had gone into the barn to put their horses away, and Don was nowhere to be seen. I tried to pull myself up enough to get off the saddle horn, but gravity took over and I couldn't do it. I then attempted to pull my leg up to get back on the horse, but I couldn't do that, either. I even tried reaching over to hold on to the other side of the saddle and pull myself up, but that didn't work.

I looked down and saw I was still at least three feet off the ground. So I scrambled a bit more, which got my shirt tangled up around the saddle horn. Then I started to panic. If Dusty took off on a wild gallop, I could be strangled. (Dusty probably had not galloped in years, but I wasn't thinking clearly at this point.)

My husband finally noticed me in limbo on this gargantuan horse and came over to ask me what I was doing.

*What am I doing?* I wanted to scream. *What does it look like I'm doing?! I'm hanging off a horse by my bra, and I'm worried about being strangled, or worse, making church history. (Remember that time Lilly accidentally turned horseback riding into a topless event?)*

However, Don stood talking to me from the other side of the horse, so I couldn't answer him. I finally got his attention and asked him to push me back on the horse. He refused, thinking maybe I changed my mind and wanted to go again or something.

And all the time I was struggling, scrambling, and panicking, Dusty just stood still. I flailed around, aimlessly swinging my legs and arms, trying to find something that worked, and she just stood there.

Linda finally came back. After appraising the situation, she told me to calm down. Then she instructed me to put my foot in the stirrup and use that to push myself up, which enabled me to get untangled, dismounted, and redressed before I ran into the rest of the group. In my frazzled state, I'd never even noticed the stirrup.

After getting down, I patted Dusty and thanked her for the ride. Not the least eventful horseback ride I'd ever had, but it was still a great experience. From Dusty, I learned this amazing thing about peace: the more I flail around, the more tangled up I get.

Usually, the more out of control my life gets, the more stressed I become. Then I try to figure things out on my own. How this horse could stand peacefully through all my wiggling was beyond me, but I knew that the Bible teaches us that true peace is in Christ. Dusty, with her calmness and patience, taught me the true meaning of Philippians 4:7: "And the peace of God, which transcends all understanding, will guard your hearts and minds in Christ Jesus."

So after my fateful ride, I started to pray for that peace that surpasses all understanding. Over the next few years we faced some difficult situations, but God provided an amazing peace throughout them all.

I learned a life lesson from a horse—a horse that stood still.

*Lilly Allison is a freelance writer from Irving, Texas. Married with two grown children, she is a CLASS graduate, Certified Personality Trainer, and member of the Christian Writers Guild. She can be reached at lattelal@yahoo.com.*

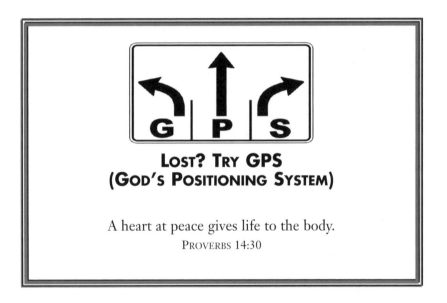

## LOST? TRY GPS
## (GOD'S POSITIONING SYSTEM)

A heart at peace gives life to the body.
PROVERBS 14:30

## WHERE'S BILLY?

God assured us, "I'll never let you down, never walk off and leave you."
HEBREWS 13:5 MSG

"Where's Billy?!" my mom asked, concern etched across her forehead.

My mom, dad, two brothers, and I were on a cross-country road trip. We had just made a pit stop at a gas station in the deserts of Nevada. While we slept, Dad filled the tank.

Now my other brother, Checker, gave a panicked exclamation. "He's not here!"

Pandemonium broke out. Dad cast a quick glance in the rearview mirror and pulled over, not believing that their firstborn son was actually missing. Sure enough, Billy wasn't anywhere in the car. Not on the red vinyl seat, not asleep on the floor ... not anywhere!

Dad swerved the steering wheel hard to the left and made our '57 cherry-red station wagon careen back from whence it came. Eyes trained on the horizon, Mom and Dad searched for a first glimpse of the gas station. As they drew nearer to it, Checker was the first to say, "There he is!"

Eight-year-old Bill, leaning against a pole, looked completely unruffled. He even gave a little yawn.

After much hugging and kissing, we learned that while Dad filled the tank, Bill had slipped out of the car in a sleepy stupor and shuffled off to the bathroom.

Mom noticed Billy's calm demeanor and asked, "Were you scared?"

He casually—almost flippantly—said, "Nope. I knew you'd come back."

Yes, it's admirable that an eight-year-old remained calm when he came out from the bathroom and his family's vehicle was gone. But why did he remain so composed, almost serene? He *knew* beyond a shadow of a doubt that his parents would come back for him. He *knew* their track record—and they had never failed him.

When we feel as if we've been left behind by God in the Nevada desert and our prayers seem to bounce right off the gas station's bathroom ceiling, let's remind ourselves of God's faithfulness. Has he ever left us behind for good?

Sometimes God will leave us in tough predicaments to see how we'll react. We've got to remember his track record and his promises. And we, like Billy, will have the peace that passes understanding.

# An Uncommon Bond

KATHY CLENNEY, AS TOLD TO DENA DYER

Sisters share clothes, friends, rooms, cars, dates—even boyfriends. But my sister and I share a bond we never expected and would never have asked for.

In 1993, during a routine physical, I heard some shocking news. "Something is wrong with your kidneys," the doctor said.

At first, I wasn't too worried. After all, I didn't have any symptoms of kidney disease. But for three years, I underwent a battery of tests, my charts passed from physician to confused physician, and my health deteriorated. Finally, a nephrologist (kidney specialist) discovered the root of my problems.

After a biopsy, I learned I had less than 10 percent of my kidney functions.

During those traumatic years, I prayed for strength, hope, and peace. One night, I even asked my husband, Travis, to pray that I'd die. I hurt terribly. A walk to the mailbox was a big deal. At night, my legs cramped so severely I barely slept at all. And food—just to smell it made me sick.

In February 1997 I went on dialysis. My specialist, Dr.

Chary, recommended that I consider becoming a kidney transplant recipient.

At first, I was adamant that no one give his or her kidney to save me. I thought I could live with dialysis, but after I went through the treatments for a while, I realized the quality of life wasn't really better than what I already had. It wasn't much of a life at all.

I just didn't know what to do.

Finally, I gave consent for close family members to be tested for a match. But my son wasn't eligible, and my daughter was pregnant. Then my older sister, Nancy, offered to be tested.

Initially, I said no. I knew that the surgery was dangerous—especially for someone in middle age—and the recovery time was much longer for the donor than the recipient.

So Nancy prayed and waited. And just as I decided to have my name added to the national transplant list, she called me. "It could be a very long wait," she said. "Please, please, let me give you my kidney. I want to do it!"

Even now—five healthy years later—I cry when I remember how Nancy persuaded me. She revealed that our daddy, on his deathbed, had made her promise to "take care of Kat." She wanted to keep her promise. We had grown up poor, and I had contracted rheumatic fever as a child. Nan had always felt protective of me—even more so after Father pleaded with her to watch over her baby sister.

Nancy knew the risks. Her husband, Terry, was really supportive, but her eldest son was scared. I worried, too, but Nancy's insistence on keeping her word to Daddy finally convinced me to relent. And once we made the decision to go through with the surgery, I just knew everything would be okay. God gave me an incredible sense of peace—I felt as if he held me up the whole time. It was as if he were saying, "You're both going to be okay. I have it all under control." And Nan and I have always been so much alike—the way we think, act, dress—that I knew her kidney would suit me just fine. So on April 25, 1997, we checked in to a hospital in Memphis, Tennessee, and began the arduous transplant process.

In addition to similar genetic makeup, Nancy and I share a sense of humor. Following the procedure, we were wheeled into the same recovery room and lay side by side on separate gurneys as we came out of anesthesia. We got to laughing so hard about our pitiful conditions that it hurt. They almost had to separate us.

I felt confident even after initial blood tests (immediately following the procedure) showed I might be rejecting my sister's organ. At that time, Nancy felt horrible—that perhaps she hadn't helped me after all. Making things worse was our knowledge of a recent Nashville transplant patient who had rejected her new organ.

However, my faith in God—and belief that things would turn out okay for both of us—was confirmed when my blood levels stabilized, and both Nancy and I healed quite quickly.

One thing that makes Nancy's sacrifice remarkable is her humility. "To me," she said, "it was like you asked me for a loaf of bread, not an organ."

But she saved my life!

Nancy simply said, "You're my sister. There was never a question of whether or not I'd go through with it."

When I ponder the immensity of her gift and the health challenges that led me to the transplant, I realize how much I've learned. I'd always been good at giving, but I had to learn to receive. Don't get me wrong—it was hard. But my favorite

Bible verse is the one where Paul said that God's strength is made perfect in our weakness.

Thanks to the strength of the Lord and skilled surgeons, we two sisters, who have already shared so much—faith, a hard childhood, and a silly sense of humor—now share good health as well as an uncommon story of strength, hope, and peace.

*Kathy Clenney is a wife, mom, and grandmother who lives in Jackson, Tennessee. She remains in good health. Praise the Lord!*

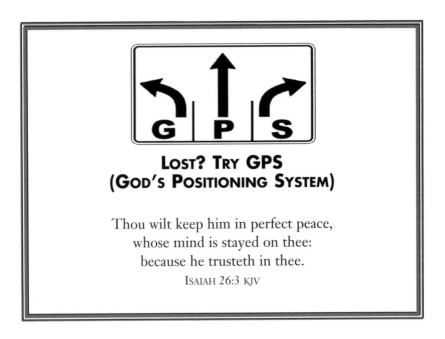

## Lost? Try GPS (God's Positioning System)

Thou wilt keep him in perfect peace,
whose mind is stayed on thee:
because he trusteth in thee.
Isaiah 26:3 kjv

## PART TWO

# BIG GIRLS DON'T CRY
# (Peace with Others)

# Football Follies

DENA DYER

I love autumn in Texas. After a summer of perspiring through all my T-shirts, I breathe a sigh of relief as temperatures cool, school supplies go on sale, and the days begin to shorten. I take out my flannel pajamas—hoping to use them by Christmas. And I wait for the real highlight of the season to begin.

Each night as I lie in bed, visions dance in my head—not of sugarplums, but of greasy corndogs and Frito pies. I dream of high school marching bands flitting around fifty-yard lines.

That's right ... fall in Texas is all about two words—*foot* and *ball*.

However, even while I'm salivating at the thought of concession stand goodies, my unique "not a sports fan" husband flips through the television channels. He tries desperately to find one station that hasn't lengthened its sports coverage by thirty minutes (it really irks him, too, that they rename the sports section of the news and give it a separate theme song). "What IS it with these people?" Carey asks.

He forgets that I am one of them. I try to be civil as I explain to Carey the hold football has on my home state. However, his brain—warped by too many glasses of sweet tea—can't quite wrap around it.

My dear hubby simply doesn't understand the thrill of Friday-night games full of coaches, cornerbacks, and cheerleaders. Maybe it comes from too many nights spent on smelly school buses when he was a high school trumpet player. Perhaps he still sees football from a band member's perspective: the game is too long, and the athletes are snotty to the band nerds.

And then I try to explain the concept of "the homecoming game." You see, in Texas, a gal lives for the moment she gets asked to her first homecoming football game. In a state known for burly men, big hair, and beauty queens, this special night combines it all into one gigantic, gaudy package.

The festivities begin with a week of pregame activity at all the local schools. Students compete in spirit contests for locker and hall decorating, dress in crazy costumes, and attend bonfires and parades. All week long, high school students talk about for whom they're voting as homecoming king and queen and whom they're taking to the postgame dance.

My junior year, I told my buddy Chad I would go with him on one condition—that he didn't spend a lot of money on a mum. In Texas, boys buy corsages as big as an oil mogul's ten-gallon hat for their dates. The girls reciprocate with the gift of a garter (the kind single guys clamor for after weddings). But these corsages—called "mums"—aren't just any old works of floral craftsmanship.

Under the mums and garters are streamers full of sparkly stickers, miniature cowbells, football helmets, feathers, and even a number of "extras"—including twinkle lights and music boxes. The biggest mums can set guys back hundreds of dollars. I knew I didn't want a friend spending that kind of money on me. And because Chad wasn't someone I was trying to impress, I even decided to go with a homemade garter for him. I affixed all sorts of little goodies to it with staples (this was before hot glue became my weapon of choice).

I felt quite proud of myself when I looked at the finished product. I'd saved a few bucks, and it still looked nice. Chad would be none the wiser—or so I thought.

However, by the second quarter of the game, the garter began to unravel. By the third quarter, we were covered with glitter, feathers, and staples. It looked like we'd been attacked by a Vegas chicken.

"I hope you didn't spend a lot on this," he finally said. "Whoever made it for you sure didn't do a very good job."

I mumbled something about how "you sure don't get much for your money these days." Then I excused myself to go to the bathroom, where I laughed and cried for several minutes.

I should have told Chad the truth that night, but I wasn't mature enough. Years later, I'm ashamed and embarrassed that I didn't.

Since then, I've been known to cut other corners. I tend to drive too fast, seldom dust my furniture, and usually don't have backup plans when things go wrong.

I also hate to say it, but I tend to try and maintain my friendships with e-mails and short phone calls. That's better than not communicating at all, but it's not the best way to encourage others to invest in a long-term relationship. If I'm not putting the time in, why should they?

I even cut corners spiritually. Instead of spending thirty minutes with God each day, I sometimes try to keep my spiritual life going on "Help, Lord!" prayers and five-minute devotional readings, sandwiched in between phone calls, church activities, and pediatrician appointments. And while I know my relationship to God is not based on performance, I also know that I'm the one who misses out when I choose that sort of drive-through approach to spirituality.

So I'm making a resolution this football season: to try to quit cutting corners in the important areas of my life. I may not dust a lot more this year, but I want to give people (and the Lord) the quality time and attention they deserve. Pray for me, will you? I'm gonna need it!

And just so you know, my homecoming story is not without a happy ending. I think I changed the course of Chad's life. Really!

Recently, I read a magazine from my old hometown that featured prominent businesspeople. Chad was one of them. And I promise I'm not making this up: the person I shared those "football follies" with is now (drum roll, please) ... a florist.

I guess mum's the word.

**FAVORITE OFFBEAT ROAD TRIP EXITS**

**Midpoint Café, Adrian, Texas**—Step back into time as you enter this charming little café, located at the geo-mathematical center of the famous Route 66. When you stop in for its juicy, old-fashioned burgers, be sure to say "hey" to Fran and Joann!

**Cadillac Ranch, near Amarillo, Texas**—Ten 1949–1963 Cadillacs are buried nose-deep into the Texas dirt and spray-painted in bright colors. Totally kitschy!

# Don't Be a Drip

RHONDA RIZZO WEBB

We made our first home in a darling fairy-tale cottage complete with green shutters, a manicured lawn brimming with glorious lavender and scarlet blossoms, and, what else?—a picket fence. It was meticulously decorated and just right for a newly married couple. Except for a slightly leaky roof, our cottage was cozy and perfect.

Whenever it rained, however, our den became an obstacle course of pots and pans, towels and buckets. The constant dripping made it almost impossible to spend time in that part of the house. The incessant drip-drip-drip, plip-plop-plip-plop echoed ceaselessly in my ears. Nothing could control it, short of replacing the entire roof. We constantly hoisted heavy, sopping wet towels and replaced them with dry ones—only to have to replace them again almost immediately. Wringing towels, emptying buckets, stalking each fledgling leak, plip-plop-plip-plop ... I wanted to stop the madness!

That old house reminded me of the verse, "A constant

dripping on a day of steady rain and a contentious woman are alike" (Prov. 27:15 NASB).

Unfortunately, sometimes that's me! Every time I nag my poor husband, Jimmy, I am like a constant dripping. Drip, drip, drip.

In our current home, a breakfast bar divides our kitchen and den. Jimmy's things seem to accumulate there because of its central location. Tonight, for example, the bar is littered with an old newspaper, a printed e-mail message, miscellaneous opened mail, a tape recorder, a video camera, a number of Post-it Notes with various reminders, an old name tag, a stack of charts and files, an empty plastic tool box, a cell phone, and a pager.

Looking at this clutter all day long every day would drive many women nuts! And it drove me crazy for years. I complained about it continually. Or, worse, I'd try to clean it up for him. In my earnest desire to be a helpmate, I provided pretty wicker baskets for him to stack everything in. I created neat, organized piles in an effort to make his life easier. But all my efforts just disgusted him and made him angry and distant. What's up with that?!

Then, one day, I figured out that that is just the way he works. He needs his clutter. He cleans it up whenever we are expecting guests, and if guests arrive unexpectedly, then, so what? They can see the mess.

You know what I realized? His happiness is so much more valuable to me than a clean breakfast bar. And asking him over and over to clean it up will only make him unhappy and cause friction in our home. First Corinthians 13:5 says that love "is not self-seeking." When I habitually harp around the house, demanding my own way, I am a nag. Or to put it another way, I'm a drip!

God taught me that if I must ask Jimmy to do something, I should ask just once. Oh, and God said, *ask nicely.* If Jimmy doesn't take care of that particular need, so be it. I must do the right thing by obeying God and not complaining! Then, I need to trust God to handle the rest. God may choose to convict my husband that he is not doing what he should. Or, God may choose to convict me that I never should have asked him to do it in the first place. Either way, I need to just trust God to handle it. Nagging is the same as not trusting God.

So, now I try to make my request known only once—and nicely! If the need or desire is not fulfilled, God knows that either I don't really need it, or I can handle it myself. Whatever the case, it may not be for me to know or understand. Still, God promises that he will take care of me.

I can trust him! Talk about peace!

What's the moral to my story? Trust God. Don't be a drip!

*Rhonda Webb is a conference speaker and author of* Words Begin in Our Hearts *(Moody, 2003). She lives with her husband, Jim, and children, Jimmy and Scout, in peaceful northeast Oklahoma. Visit her at www.rhondawebb.com.*

## STARSHINE'S HOW'S YOUR INNERSTATE?

### Focusing on Contentment/Gratitude

Are there things in your marriage that cause you to struggle with contentment? What contributes (or could contribute) to possessing an "attitude of gratitude" in your relationship?

Has the Lord ever blessed you and/or your spouse as a result of changing your attitude? Journal about a specific example.

Ask the Lord how he wants you to step out of your comfort zone and courageously trust him in this area of your life. Then listen to what he says, and ask him to help you obey. Jesus reminds us in John 15 that apart from him we can do nothing. As we avail ourselves of his strength, wisdom, and power, we become all he wants us to be.

# WE'RE ALL GROWN-UPS HERE

BECKY FREEMAN AND RUTHIE ARNOLD
ADAPTED FROM *HELP! I'M TURNING INTO MY
MOTHER: WITH A FEW QUIRKS OF MY OWN*

While in her early thirties, my sister, Rachel, went through some intense and private inner struggles. She felt that part of her pain had to do with some of the ways my folks dealt with her as she grew up, particularly in the area of discipline.

We all knew how much Mother, especially, wanted to maintain closeness in our family now that we kids were married adults with children. In order to give Mother this closeness—real closeness, not based on performance—Rachel felt she needed to have a heart-to-heart talk with my parents about some of these old wounds.

From her home in Virginia, she painstakingly crafted a letter to my parents in Texas and called to tell them it was on the way. "You've asked me, Mom, if there was something between us, and I've said no. But the truth is, there are some things I think we need to deal with."

Looking back on this now, I see what terrific courage it took for my sister to risk being honest. But at the time, I feared Mother might keel over in a dead faint, fall into a bottomless pit

**111**

of deep depression, or worse. Generally, *my* motto in life is "Let sleeping dogs lie." In other words, "If it ain't broke past working, don't fix it!" As the consummate people-pleasing pacifist, I felt like crawling into a foxhole, putting both fingers in my ears, and waiting there until it was all over.

But—to my surprise and relief—a beautiful thing happened. That courageous act led to a peaceful reconciliation with both my mom and dad.

The letter arrived in Texas. Within a few days, Daddy had the opportunity to be in Virginia on a business trip that he extended in order to spend some time with Rachel. For three days, Daddy and Rachel spent time in coffee shops and talked about the past over lunch. (Never underestimate coffee-shop therapy). Finally, on a deserted park bench by the ocean, they held each other and cried. And Rachel was able to understand why he had done some of the things he had done and to forgive my dad.

Then came Mother's turn to make the trip to Virginia. On the next-to-last day of Mother's visit, she and Rachel pulled into the driveway after a visit to the grocery store, and the floodgates opened.

Being women, their tears started immediately, but there were never any harsh words. Some of what Mother told Rachel helped her to see that as the adult child of an alcoholic parent, Mother brought her own wounds and defenses into parenting.

Finally, while they held each other, Mother said through tears, "You are so right about so many of those things. I was young, and I was selfish, too, at times. But it was never because I didn't love you, honey! Please know you were such a joy to us, and you've been so much fun to raise. I am SO proud of you!"

And Rachel, bless her heart, sobbed out the healing words

Mother also badly needed to hear. "I know, Mom. I love you, too. And I do forgive you."

Finally, I knew my own phone call had to be made. Mother answered on the third ring, and after a few words, I managed to say what I had called to say.

"Mother, ever since you've worked through some things with Rachel, you've asked me several times if there was anything we needed to talk about, and I've said no. But ... there *are* some things, and I just don't think the two of us can get through them ourselves. Would you consider working with a family counselor?"

"Of course!" she responded. "Let's do it!"

I felt a therapist might help me put what I was feeling into words—much of it had to do with becoming "my own person" as all daughters have to do. I think God used even the pain of my escaping the desperate need of consistent, 100 percent approval from my mother in order to make both of us into healthier women, as well as make our relationship much more real, peaceful, and fun.

And then we came to the really BIG problem. We'd chosen a therapist in Dallas, halfway between Mother's house in Bedford and my house in Greenville. How were the two of us independent, capable women going to navigate the unfamiliar terrain of North Dallas, and particularly the frantic North Dallas Tollway?

We both managed, but when we met in the parking lot at the counselor's office, I couldn't help asking, "How many extra quarters did *you* have to pay before you got off at the right exit?"

"Three," she admitted, grinning. "What about you?"

"Two!" I announced triumphantly.

We made that harrowing trip about three times before the

garbage and cobwebs that had accumulated in hidden places of our relationship were swept away. Some cobwebs had been there a long time, while others were more recent. There had been misunderstandings on both sides, most of which evaporated once we could be honest and open with each other. On one particularly emotional day, the tears and words flowed in torrents from both of us, leading up to a scene that would have made any movie director proud. At the end of the storm, we fell into each other's arms, crying, "I love you!" The counselor, a woman about my age, watched us with eyes as big as silver dollars and with a grin that said, "I don't think I've ever seen a mother and daughter quite like you two."

Interestingly, Mother later told both Rachel and me that this was one of the hardest but most helpful times of her life, and she thanked us for it. "I marvel," she said, "that the two of you loved me enough to open your hearts and to risk hearing my heart as well. To be honest, it was excruciatingly hard at times, but I knew in my heart of hearts that Christ was doing a long-awaited work in my life at a time I was ready to receive it. I felt him very near through it all, and I spent lots of time in prayer through those hard days.

"Honestly trying to look at what you are, what you have been, the mistakes you have made—well, it's terrifying and so very humbling. Shame and guilt rush in like a flood at times, especially in the areas where you feel you've failed your children. At the same time, I considered it a wonderful opportunity and a great privilege—a chance to know myself better, to change, and to grow. I had nothing to lose except pride."

When I asked Mom how she'd gotten through that tough time (I foresaw a few hard days in my own future, since I have five kids!), she said, "First of all, I asked the Holy Spirit to guide my words through it all and to help me do anything I could to help both of you experience more freedom in your lives. I asked him to make our family a place where honesty and openness with each other was much easier than it had been. And I prayed that he would not let this time of working through the pain end before I was what and where he wanted me to be." She stopped and smiled. "I think it's called 'sanctification'—the Spirit chiseling away, making us more and more like Christ. Bless him; he just will not let us stay the same! At least, not comfortably."

Since that time, my own grown children and I have been through a few counseling sessions. And this time, *I* got a taste of what it's like to be the mama under the microscope and to hear the ways I'd caused my children pain. It was not easy, to say the least. But to have the chance—to respond to my kids' woundedness, to say how much I loved them, how I blew it, how immature I was at times—was a blessed privilege, and it took my relationship with them to a new level of peace and understanding.

Henri Nouwen compared the maturing of our lives to the sacrament of the Communion bread: we are taken, broken, blessed—and then given. Perhaps nowhere else is this process more evident than within our all-too-human families. And perhaps nowhere else is it as much worth the effort.

*Becky Freeman is the award-winning author of* Worms in My Tea and Other Mixed Blessings *(Broadman and Holman, 1994) and many other books. A speaker much in demand nationally, she makes her home in Colorado. Visit www.beckyfreeman.com for more information.*

*Ruthie Arnold, who lives in Granbury, Texas, wrote both* Help!

I'm Turning into My Mother: With a Few Quirks of My Own *(Harvest House, 2002) and the bestselling* Worms in My Tea and Other Mixed Blessings *with her daughter Becky Freeman.*

**LOST? TRY GPS
(GOD'S POSITIONING SYSTEM)**

Make every effort to keep the unity of the
Spirit through the bond of peace.
EPHESIANS 4:3

# A Vacation Like No Other

HEATHER ENRIGHT

Aren't vacations wonderful? Who doesn't love the thrill of escaping the daily grind of day-to-day chores, obligations, and demands? Of course, I have learned an important, albeit discouraging, lesson about vacations since I became a mother. Traveling with your children is not a vacation, at least not in that luxurious, relaxing sense of the word. Instead of escaping the norm, we get to experience it all in a new setting, which can actually be more stressful. Yet, for the sake of family memories and fun, we moms take it in stride. We take one for the team.

Despite knowing how stressful vacations can be, I began our last one with high hopes. For months, we'd planned a ski trip—the first for our two sons, ages three and five. My husband's father, stepmother, and sisters would be coming, too. I figured that between the six of us, my children would be well-entertained. And, since I was five months pregnant, I would just have to stay in the condo all day, alone, on my own leisurely timetable while everyone else skied. As I said, sometimes you have to take one for the team.

On that first day of the vacation, my husband and I took the boys to ski school, and then he set off for a glorious day of spring skiing. I gleefully headed back to the hotel room, nearly overwhelmed by the idea of quiet and solitude. My mind raced with all the things I could do, and I couldn't quite decide which task to accomplish first. *Or maybe,* I thought, *I should just accomplish nothing.* After all, my husband is constantly saying that for me, relaxing *is* an accomplishment.

I felt a sudden conviction that I ought to start by having a prolonged time with the Lord, taking advantage of the rare opportunity to read my Bible and pray as long as I might like. I knew instantly that it was a call for obedience. But I rationalized that I could do that later—this was my time, and I would relax in front of the television first. So I turned on the tube and began channel surfing.

I stopped on one station featuring Beth Moore being interviewed by James Robison. She was saying that in order for believers to have freedom in Christ, they have to work through their past. "He cannot become Lord of the 'is to come' in our life," she said, "until he has become Lord of 'what was.'"

Five days earlier, I had heard those exact words while watching a Beth Moore video lecture with my Bible study class.

God had my full attention.

My husband and I have often laughed about how our children will choose the same video or library book time after time. We find it amusing (and sometimes annoying) when they demand we sing the same song for the twelfth time in a row. In any event, what is true of them is true of me—we learn through repetition.

God had been dealing with me about my past for months at this point. For about a year, every sermon topic, Sunday school class, or Bible study seemed to address moving through past hurts. It was time to listen up and learn, once and for all.

Like many people, I had been hurt by those I hold most dear, the people who were supposed to love and nurture me. For many years, I struggled with feeling worthless, rejected, bitter, and angry. I had been the queen of the pity party, justifying my anger and wallowing in my poor, unfortunate circumstances.

At times, the pain had been great enough to inhibit my daily functioning. The anger and fear of being hurt again had caused me to build a wall and made me quick to push off relationships before I could get hurt again. I had bought the lie—that I was damaged goods—hook, line, and sinker. It was time for a change.

As soon as Beth Moore finished speaking, I grabbed my Bible and prayer journal. In the silence of the hotel room, I began to consider all my past hurts, taking careful inventory of the issues that needed to be laid to rest. My mind went back through two decades and numerous conversations, assumptions, and encounters. I wrote them all down, facing my struggles head on.

Then, God gave me eyes to see the pieces of the puzzle and how they all fit together. He reminded me that he was there in the middle of each painful circumstance. We went through each hurt together, one by one. I was challenged to accept, by faith, that the Lord was there in the middle of it all and that he had never abandoned me. I had to acknowledge that fact, believing and trusting that he desired the best for me.

And I had to choose. Would those hurts define me or *refine* me? Who did I want to be—a victim dragging around my baggage, hoping to evoke everyone's attention? Or a victorious overcomer who finds fulfillment knowing that God has my best interests at heart? Will I try to get sympathy or be freed to grant others compassion?

Finally, I sat back, exhausted by the mental and emotional exercise and looked out the window. I saw the pristine, white snow, nearly glowing with the midday sunshine of early spring. Huge banks of untouched powder appeared perfect without a trace of a single footprint. They were pretty to look at but not at all useful. Being unable to calculate their depth, no one wanted to venture there. However, just a few yards away lay the path the hotel guests took from the hotel to the ski lift. Frequent use had beaten it down. It may not have looked as perfect, but it, too, shone white and bright, reflecting the sunshine just as well as the snowbanks did.

*It's the picture of my life,* I thought. Without the pain I'd been through, I was like the snowbanks. Their depths were unknown, and my usefulness to God had been questionable, regardless of how I might have appeared on the outside. Like the crushing footsteps that pushed down the snow to create a useful path, my pain had served the same purpose in my life.

My circumstances had packed down my pride, selfishness, and lack of fortitude. I'd learned to empathize with others and appreciate their needs. I'd learned the depth of my coping skills, and most importantly, I'd learned that people will always fail to meet my every expectation. Instead of being constantly disappointed in others, I can now choose to see their shortcomings as a reminder of God's faithfulness. I can be assured that he will always exceed my expectations.

And most importantly, I can be thankful for each and every painful moment that can now allow me to be used by God.

When I boarded that plane for vacation, I hoped the trip would be a retreat from my daily grind. Little did I know it would bring a permanent vacation from emotional baggage and a lasting escape from the grind of a painful past.

That day, I listened and made my choice: I'd much rather be a useful path than a pristine snowbank.

*Heather Enright and her husband, Chris, have three children— Collin, Cooper, and Caris. Aside from writing, Heather enjoys designing stationery, painting, and running her own home business, Bullfrogs and Butterflies. In her free time, she enjoys scrapbooking and sleeping.*

## God's Purple Mountain Majesty

**PEPPER'S PIT STOPS**

"You will seek me and find me when you
seek me with all your heart."
JEREMIAH 29:13

After many years of dreaming about visiting Glacier National Park, the day finally arrived. We planned on camping and heard that Many Glacier Campground had the best views and sold out quickly. Nonetheless, we decided to try to secure a campsite at Many Glacier on the opposite end of the park before all spots were taken for the night. After racing over mountain and stream, we arrived at Many Glacier with only three campsites remaining. We quickly snatched one up.

When I wondered out loud about what that cute, little

building—located right smack in front of us on our campsite—could be, my husband informed me it was the RV "dump station."

I had *really* looked forward to a getting-back-to-God-and-nature vacation, but this "dump station" was something else. I hate to admit it, but it got to me ... bad. I sulked around, grumbling, "I can't believe we're finally in this beautiful park, and all we can see is this *dump* station!"

But then Kailey crawled up in my lap, and said, "Mommy, look! You can *still* see the mountains from here!"

Though still pouting, I realized a spiritual lesson was taking shape.

How many other times had I let small, inconsequential dump station-like problems get in the way of enjoying God's plan for me? Such circumstances can look huge, blocking out God's artistic arrangement for our lives. But what would happen if I looked *beyond* the dump station stuff?

As I sat there on the worn picnic table, eating humble pie, I tilted my head just slightly. And there it was. I could still see it: God's purple mountain majesty.

# FROM PEST TO BEST FRIEND

SUSAN MYERS

I didn't want a baby sister. Although I liked the fact my mother was going to have another baby, I didn't want it to be a girl. My brother and I each had a bedroom of our own, and whether the baby was a boy or girl would determine which sibling would go from a single to a double.

I lost.

I remember trying to convince my mother that as the oldest I should have my own room, and that it wasn't fair for me to have to share. It didn't work. The crib moved in and with it, an occupant who loved to get the whole household up in the middle of the night. I soon found that putting the covers over my head and stuffing my fingers in my ears didn't do anything to quell the blast of our new air raid siren.

I guess I grew to like her. But with a six-year age difference, I knew we would never have anything in common. Besides, she didn't make it easy with her attitude of "what's your is mine." And if she broke something, it became my fault because I should have known better than to leave it where she could get her hands on it.

Things weren't destined to get any fairer. I remember one night when she was about two and wouldn't to go to bed unless I came, too.

"She wants to be with you because she loves you," my mother said.

*No, she doesn't,* I thought. *She just wants to make me miserable.* As I lay there in my bed, pretending to be asleep so the little rug rat would give in and drift off, I wondered what I had done to deserve such a trial. (Not until several years later would I figure out it wasn't what I had done, but what my parents had done!)

But it was done, and I could see no one waiting around to take the little darling back.

As she grew older, my brother and I found her a convenient target.

"You're adopted," we told her once when she was seven. Our parents had gone to the store and not-so-wisely left us in charge of our little sister.

"No, I'm not," she shouted back.

"Yes, you are," we insisted. "Mom and Dad found you on the side of the road and felt sorry for you."

I don't think she ever really believed us, but she did check with Mom and Dad when they returned, just to be sure. Our parents never left us alone much after that.

We spent the rest of our childhood uttering phrases with the power to drive any mother mad.

"I'm telling."

"She hit me."

"She's lying."

As the oldest, I was supposed to be the mature one. I didn't see that as fair *at all.*

Although we still didn't have much in common, I occasionally felt twinges of jealousy as I watched my siblings play. I remember them using sheets to build a fort out of the living room furniture, something I considered myself too old to participate in. My brother was closer to my age, and my sister and I were both girls. Shouldn't that give us some kind of bond?

But instead of bonding, we called each other names.

"Spoiled rotten."

"Bossy!"

So how, I wonder now, did the ultimate pest turn into my dearest friend?

The change didn't start until after I married. She would come to spend the night, and I found that instead of remaining a pest, she'd actually turned into someone with whom I could have a conversation. But still, she was only my kid sister.

I gave birth to my son in my late twenties, and she had her daughter while in her early twenties. Our babies ended up being just fourteen months apart. Motherhood is a bond that can draw even the most diverse women together. For sisters who have shared a lifetime already, it's a miracle that unites.

We had a lot to talk about.

"Does he look like our side of the family or Joel's?"

"I can remember when you did the same thing at her age!"

Suddenly it was fun to hang around my baby sister. We dressed our little darlings in costumes and took them to "Haunt the Zoo." We sympathized over temper tantrums (the kids', not ours) and weight gain, and we shared ideas on how to cope. We went from "I'm telling" to "I'll never tell."

We still don't have all the same interests. But she puts up with my dragging her through craft stores with only minimal whining. She has also come to terms with my lack of directional skills and usually takes the helm for any navigational adventures.

As a counterpoint, I put up with her calling before coming to my house only to ask, "What are you going to feed me?"

Instead of telling her to "take it or leave it" as I do my family, I plan a menu for her. After all, she's my baby sister.

I realized how much our relationship had changed while on a weekend trip the two of us took, sans families. We stayed in a beautiful cabin, rustic right down to the fact that it didn't have a television. We could have spent the evenings reading the books we two avid readers had toted to the cabin. But instead, we bought a deck of cards and talked. Over games of gin rummy, double solitaire, and even the old children's game war, we talked.

And we talked and talked—about our families, dreams for the future, where to go the next day, even what we thought about the nearby motorcycle convention.

Is she still a spoiled rotten little sister? Am I still a bossy older sister?

Yep ... but after thirty-plus years of traveling life's road together—watching out for the potholes, slowing down for the bumps, and keeping an eye out for the sharp curves—she's more than a pest.

She's my best friend.

*Susan Meyers lives in Oklahoma with her husband, son, and one spoiled cat. She is the author of several published short stories. You can learn more about Susan at her Web site: www.members.cox.net/sameyers/Main.*

**FAVORITE OFFBEAT ROAD TRIP EXITS**

**Mount St. Helens, Washington**—Our family thought a stop here would be brief, but we ended up staying the entire day at this natural disaster-turned-National Volcanic Monument. Fascinating!

**Hyder, Alaska**—This remote town of one hundred is the southernmost town in Alaska accessible by road. It shares an International Chamber of Commerce with its Canadian neighbor, Stewart, British Columbia, and the bank is open only three days a week, three hours a day. Eagles, glaciers, and bears, oh my!

# POSITIVE PEACE WITH SLIGHTLY IMPERFECT PEOPLE

KAROL LADD

T-shirt reading is a big sport of mine. It's rather amusing to discover great truths and funny quips on the backs of people as they stroll through the mall.

Recently, I spotted a lady wearing a shirt that read, "To err is human; to forgive is canine." It's a sad day when a trait that should be evident in *our* lives is actually found to a greater extent in the family dog. Now don't get me wrong. I adore my dogs, but I do believe God intended the qualities of love and forgiveness to be recognizable traits in his people.

However, it's not easy to forgive—which is probably where the T-shirt's author was coming from. Forgiveness is a great concept until we have to practice it ourselves!

My first big opportunity to dole out a large portion of forgiveness was in junior high back in 1973. My best friend Agnes (not her real name) began making fun of me behind my back. She took my words and twisted them to make me sound like a goofball. She joked about my clothes because I didn't have the coolest colors of army/navy jeans. And she even pointed out the humor in the way I ate my cheese puffs during lunchtime.

Agnes was my soul mate one minute and my enemy the next. She was the Lucy to my Charlie Brown. When I finally discovered her deception, I did what any self-respecting eighth-grade girl would do—I ran home and cried. When I finished crying, I realized I needed to confront Agnes, so, bravely, I had my mother call her mother. Some confrontation! Nonetheless, Agnes apologized and promised it would never happen again.

Now I had a choice. Would I forgive my former soul mate and help restore peace between us? Would I get back at her with a major revenge plot? Or would I simply choose to hold a long-term, nasty grudge? As a Christian, I knew in my head what God wanted me to do; it was my job to forgive her because God had forgiven me of so much.

But honestly, I had a huge internal struggle. I didn't feel like forgiving her. (I didn't even want to see her at that point!) I wish I could tell you I prayed and immediately forgave Agnes. The truth is, it took days for my feelings and actions to catch up with each other. Eventually, I made the positive choice to forgive her.

Was it easy? No, I needed God's love to pour through me. Did I trust her again with my deepest, darkest secrets? No, because forgiveness doesn't mean foolishness. Forgiving Agnes simply meant that I no longer held the offense against her. I chose to promote peace, not anger and bitterness.

To err is human, and to forgive is divine. And now that I'm a little older and hopefully a lot wiser than I was in 1973, I realize I'm not perfect, you're not perfect, and Agnes is not perfect. Like discounted pantyhose, we all wear the label "slightly imperfect." We all need forgiveness from our heavenly Father and from our fellow man.

It is God's divine nature to forgive us "slightly imperfect" people. And it's our choice day by day, hour by hour, (even sometimes minute by minute!) to allow his positive peace to pour out from us.

Throughout my travels in life, I've come across many Agneses. They've arrived in many forms: difficult roommates, unkind neighbors, annoying family members, and forgetful friends. All needed a gift of peace and forgiveness. Oddly, by God's grace my forgiveness barrel has never run dry.

I try to keep in mind that relationships get groovier with the giving (let's put *that* on a T-shirt)! And I'm always a happier person when I give up the right to hold a grudge.

Granting Agnes forgiveness was one step in my journey of learning to give, even when I didn't feel like it. As the years have passed, I've stumbled along the way, but I'm thankful God used Agnes to point me in the right direction.

*Karol Ladd is an international speaker and best-selling author of more than fifteen books including* The Power of a Positive Mom *(Howard, 2001). Often referred to as "The Positive Lady," Karol inspires audiences with her message of encouragement and hope. You can learn more about Karol at www.PositiveLifePrinciples.com.*

## LOST? TRY GPS
## (GOD'S POSITIONING SYSTEM)

But the fruit of the Spirit is love, joy, peace,
patience, kindness, goodness, faithfulness,
gentleness and self-control.

GALATIANS 5:22–23

# It Was the Best of Times

M A R I T A   L I T T A U E R

"Twenty-seven miles across the sea, Catalina Island is the place for me." The old Beach Boys' song exactly echoes my sentiments. Over the last twenty years, I have been sailing off the coast of California.

My husband, Chuck, and I try to make several treks to the island each year. Even now that we live in New Mexico, we usually make the crossing at least once a year. Our favorite destination is Catalina Island for the annual jazz festival held each year in early October, but New Year's also makes an excellent sail. This year, 1998, we chose to celebrate our fifteenth anniversary with a multiday cruise to the island.

The journey to Catalina Island is typically uneventful. The mild winds hit you in the face as they come straight ashore from the island. Leaving Newport Harbor in fog, you eventually beat back and forth, finally tacking your way across the channel and pulling into Avalon Harbor just after dusk—the twinkling lights of the village beckoning you.

This trip started no differently.

Around noon we pulled out of the dock into a gray fog that enveloped Newport Harbor. It was early May, and the fog should have lifted by then, but El Niño had confused all the weather patterns. Due to our late start, we motored out of the harbor with Chuck at the wheel and me sitting on the bowsprit to watch for any oncoming boats in the haze.

Once out of the harbor, we were anxious to sail. However, there was still no sun peeking out of the muck surrounding us and not a breath of wind. We motored past Bell Buoy Number 1 and gawked at the ever-present seals sleeping all over each other at its base, despite the incessant ringing of the bell above their heads.

We moved on in the general direction of Catalina Island. My hair blew slightly. Hah! Was that wind? We quickly raised the mainsail, then the genoa. There seemed to be enough breeze to have some slight forward motion but not enough to register on the wind vane or the telltales, which hung limply from the sail stays. Thrilled to have any breeze at all, we abandoned our course and sailed for the wind. I took the wheel while Chuck took a nap.

An hour later he stirred and asked our location. I had no idea. I'd just been steering the boat to fill the sails. Pleased to be actually sailing, I had enjoyed the silence of the ocean shrouded in fog. Chuck pulled his newly acquired GPS from his pocket, got a reading, and headed below to check the charts. Moments later he resurfaced with a discouraged expression.

"Where are we?" I asked.

"Almost to Laguna Beach."

If that were our destination or even on our rum line, that would have been great news. But, in fact, it was exactly the opposite direction of where we'd planned to go. Discouraged, I climbed on the bow and dropped the sails while Chuck turned on the motor and set our course. We continued this way for several hours—trading off taking the wheel with taking a nap. After three o'clock, the day's first rays of sun began to sparkle on the ocean's smooth surface.

With the sun's emergence came our first real wind. Chuck again took the helm, and I climbed back to my usual post of hoisting the sails.

By this time, Chuck showed the first signs of seasickness. The slow bobbing through the ocean had taken its toll, so I took over, allowing him to rest. He went down below and disappeared into the head—where he remained for quite a while. In the dim light of the cabin, I saw him finally stagger out and collapse on one of the sleeping areas.

I worried about his sickness and felt glad he was able to rest, but I also knew being down below was hardly a cure for seasickness. I urged him to come topside. "I don't want to be too far from the bathroom," he moaned. "I don't think I'm seasick. I think breakfast was bad."

I shrugged. The Marriott was not likely to serve a bad breakfast, but I let him be—by now the wind had picked up.

*Now this*, I thought, *this is why I like to sail.* The sun shone, the wind blew, and no other boat was in sight. The bow crashed through the oncoming waves, and the wind blew from the perfect direction for a timely heading to Catalina Island. I was in heaven.

However, as time went on, the wind increased, the waves mounted, and I began to feel like a tiny speck in a vast and angry ocean. I looked down below. Chuck rested comfortably, rocking back and forth with each swell while I wrestled with the wind and the boat. The sun dipped low on the horizon, and the air grew brisk. I zipped my red down parka, pulled up the fur-trimmed hood, and donned my thick, red winter gloves.

The port side of the boat nearly touched the water, and I fought to keep myself upright. The waves, now white-capped and six feet high, crashed against the bow as the boat pressed through them. Sea spray hit my face repeatedly, causing me to gasp in surprise.

As I held on for my life, part of me said, *This is some of the best sailing I've ever had. I love this!* Then another wave crashed over the bow, sloshing water all over the topside and hitting me in the face. *I am going to die,* I thought.

The popular literary reference "It was the best of times. It was the worst of times" kept surfacing in my mind as I felt both exhilaration and terror.

It felt as if I had hung on for hours, loving the wind and fearing the waves. Finally, our harbor came into view. The sun had slipped over the horizon, and the lights of Avalon began to come on. I felt exhausted, thankful, and proud—all at the same time.

I hated to wake Chuck, but I thought it was time to drop the sails and begin motoring toward the harbor. Weighing my options, I headed the boat into the wind, locked down the wheel, and began the climb to the bow—hanging on for dear life. I grabbed hold of the main sheet and moved forward to begin dropping the jib. Of course, by now the boat was no longer heading into the wind, and I battled the jib as the wind threatened to rip it from my hands.

Completely focused on my task, I did not see Chuck emerge until I heard the engine roar to life. He pointed us back into the wind as I felt a huge rush of relief. I finished dropping the jib and then dropped the main.

Safely back in the cockpit, I clung to Chuck and asked what made him get up. He said, "When I was lying there, I saw your feet go by the window. I figured out what you must be trying to do, and I knew you couldn't easily do it alone."

He felt well enough to stay at the helm all the way into the harbor. I collapsed into a heap and took my well-deserved rest.

Looking back, I realize how much this day paralleled our lives. Even though I am a capable sailor, I do not want to sail alone. Neither do I want to go through life without Chuck.

In twenty-one years of marriage, we've had rough sails and calm waters, sometimes on the same day! After working through a problem, we're often thankful, proud, and exhausted. We choose to focus on the peaceful times and know that we love and need each other. When I am weak, he is strong. When he is down, I can lift him up.

Just like that day of sailing—life is better together.

*Marita Littauer is a well-known speaker and author of thirteen books, including* But Lord, I Was Happy Shallow *(Kregel, 2004). She is President of CLASServices, Inc., which provides resources, training, and promotion for speakers and authors. For more about CLASServices, go to www.classervices.com.*

**FAVORITE OFFBEAT ROAD TRIP EXITS**

**Duck Boats at Wisconsin Dells, Wisconsin—** These duck boats (amphibious vehicles) ride over land and sea through Wisconsin Dells Glacial Park and the breathtaking Grotto Island rock formations.

**Four Corners** is located at the corners of Colorado, Utah, New Mexico, and Arizona. It's fun to take a picture of the kids on hands and knees with each appendage in a different state.

## Calm as the Ocean: The Difference between Peace and Contentment

PEPPER'S PIT STOPS

**Contentment:** Feelings of happiness and contentment may be driven by our own unique personalities. Certainly, contentment can come and go according to our circumstances. In Marita's story, the waves took their boat up and down, just as those things we deal with in daily life often take us on a roller coaster of emotions. If we let them, circumstances can rule our lives.

**Peace:** Waves may have been crashing all around Marita's boat, but I'm sure the water far below was calm, much like our spirit is when we truly let God be the Lord of our lives. When unexpected circumstances hit us, we can have a peace that passes all understanding.

Last year my family experienced a very difficult financial time, which I wrote about in our Christmas letter. Listen for the difference between my contentment and my peace.

> I compare our lives right now to an ocean in the midst of a storm. Our emotions are the waves on the surface, being tossed to and fro. Sometimes the waves are up and other times they're down. Up, down, up, down … I'm getting seasick! "Stop the wave machine! I wanna

get off," I yell at no one in particular. But down deep, where no one can see, the water is calm—even in the midst of the storm. This stillness is God's peace. Yes, we've been frustrated. I've whined. I've cried. I've yelled. I've felt sorry for my talented husband and for myself. I've informed God that I'm growing very impatient. But the deeper we dive in and trust God, the less the storm affects us.

When you experience trouble, take note of that unexplainable peace down deep, and recognize it as God in your life. You may cry, whine, or feel frustrated … but know, girlfriend, that when you surrender to him, God gives a calm as still as the bottom of an ocean in a storm. And he has his hand on you.

# DRIVING WITH GOD

TRACY RASMUSSEN

## WEEK ONE

We are riding home in the car. Twins Hannah and Elizabeth, full of the exuberance of being fifteen months old and giddy from their newly perceived ability to outwit their old mom, are strapped in the backseat, happily trying to yank off the name tags they wore during the first session of story time at the library.

I sit in the front seat, my hair frizzed with sweat from what was arguably the longest thirty minutes of my life, and pray.

> Dear God,
>
> Let me get right to the point. Why is it that all the other mothers at story time have well-behaved children who sit in their laps, sing the songs, clap their hands in glee, don't bop each other on the head with the shaky-shaky rhythm eggs, don't stand right in front of the teacher and do a tap dance, and don't try

to steal the pacifiers or stuffed animals from the babies in the group?

While I'm at it, why, in fact, does Elizabeth make a beeline for the beta fish in the tank on the children's librarian's desk, her little hands cupped to catch it, while Hannah dives under the computers and attempts to rewire them?

And why, God, don't I weigh eighty-five pounds from chasing my children, who continually run in different directions?

Please God, give me the strength next week to smile sweetly as my daughters have twin temper tantrums when they have to return their shaky-shaky rhythm eggs because that song is over and Miss Danielle wants to move on to the "Bye Bye, We Love Story Time" song.

## WEEK TWO

We are running late today, and Hannah is crying in her car seat because she'd rather have a cup of milk than the stale graham cracker I fished out of the deep sea of my purse. A better mother would have anticipated the twenty-minute chase through the biography section and the flushing of each and every toilet in the bathroom.

So now I pray.

> Dear God,
> Maybe I wasn't clear enough last week. Just because I said I didn't want Hannah and Elizabeth to run out of the story time room to play with the beta fish and computers, I did not mean I wanted them to perform tap dances while Miss Danielle

attempted to sing "Head, Shoulders, Knees and
Toes." And while I appreciate the somewhat diminished cacophony of tantrums following the shaky-
shaky rhythm egg portion of story time, I had hoped
for a blanket ban on all tantrums.

Thank you, by the way, for the gracious way in
which Hannah returned her rhythm sticks to the
bucket; however, I'm not really quite sure how her
grabbing Elizabeth's sticks and running up to the top
of the riser-seats and screaming "DADIE ADA BO"
fits into your plan for her.

Please, while you're at it, God, I'd like you to
clue me in as to why Moira's mom apparently got
one perfect child who sat there today in her matching
leopard-skin dress, hat, and shoes (at least until
Hannah tried to take a bite out of them ... what is her
fascination with eating shoes, by the way? Oh, never
mind, I don't want to confuse the issues in this prayer).

Thank you also, for the very insightful advice
from Moira's mother that if I ignored my children's
tantrums, as she did the first time Moira threw a
tantrum, they'd behave. Just the way Moira did from
that moment forward. "Perfect children are trained to
be that way," Moira's mother told me, punctuating
her statement with a perfectly arched left brow.

I am perfectly exhausted.

## WEEK THREE

I'm driving the twenty minutes to my house, and I have to go
to the bathroom. My solution to last week's bathroom incident is
to avoid it altogether. Unfortunately my bladder isn't on board

with the idea. Hannah and Elizabeth nap in the backseat, and I can see their damply curled hair in the rearview mirror. Gosh, they're cute.

But still, I pray.

> Dear God,
> Well, there's good news and bad news. The good news is that Miss Danielle has not asked us to leave story time. That's about all the good news. The bad news … well, the bad news is that now I *must* ask you about Hannah's fascination with eating shoes. By the time Miss Danielle got halfway through *Dear Zoo*, Hannah attempted to yank the shoes off three babies in the front row and got pretty ticked off when I wouldn't let her. She did somehow manage to swipe a sippy cup from some child while I was trying to get Elizabeth to stop strangling Miss Danielle's story time puppet. I returned the sippy cup to its rightful owner, who gingerly placed it in her child's diaper bag, as if Hannah's crazed behavior was contagious.
> Seriously, God, I don't mean to be petulant—but why do all these other mothers seem to have it together? Do their children sit in their laps so that they can sit in judgment of me?
> Oh, I forgot one more piece of good news. Did you see the way Elizabeth took a bow after her weekly tap dance? That was cute, don't you think?

## Week Four

Spring has begun to blossom outside the car window, so I roll it down to let the sunny breeze envelop the three of us.

Hannah and Elizabeth giggle with each other in the backseat. I'd cherish the moment except I've learned that when they chortle in unison, it's a bad, bad thing. I have a hard enough time understanding baby talk. There is no Berlitz class for twinspeak.

So instead, I pray.

> Dear God,
>     I don't think we're making progress. That's all I have to say. Okay, it's not all I have to say. Hannah didn't eat any shoes today, sure, but I seriously don't know where she learned to turn up the volume on the boom box Miss Danielle uses as accompaniment to the story time songs. Hannah's kinda smart, isn't she, God? Oh, and thanks again (no, not really) for Moira's mom's insights. Today, right after Hannah and Elizabeth ran full tilt into each other in the middle of the shaky-shaky rhythm egg dance she mentioned that my daughters sure do fall down a lot. I nodded and gave her my now-famous story time strained smile and said, succinctly, "Yes, they do."
>     *It's because they actually move*, I wanted to say. So thank you for putting your hand over my mouth in that moment.

## Week Five

Next week is the last week of story time. As we drive home, I look in the backseat and see Hannah and Elizabeth sitting content and happy in their car seats. Their faces are spotted with chocolate graham cracker, a reward for not eating any shoes at all today.

However, I still need to clarify some things, so I pray.

Dear God,

Hannah full-body-checked little Rosie today. It happened when Rosie decided to join in the shaky-shaky egg dance with Hannah and Elizabeth. It was an exuberant accident, and even though I ran over to them in a flash, I was already too late. When Hannah saw Rosie crying, she started to whimper in solidarity. Elizabeth clapped for the very dramatic way in which Hannah and Rosie fell. I glanced quickly at the faces of the other mothers to see who disapproved and saw lots of knowing smiles. Thank you, God, for that. Oh, but I really could have done without the very loud raspberries Hannah and Elizabeth decided to blow during the "Bye Bye, We Love Story Time" song.

## WEEK SIX

I'm sitting here in my car grinning. Hannah and Elizabeth yell something foreign in the backseat that probably means "Hit the gas, Mommy," but I savor the moment. Oh, there was the usual story time craziness. Hannah couldn't control her newfound need to climb and spent most of the thirty minutes going up and down the stairs. Elizabeth sang one of the songs while actually sitting in my lap, though. Maybe she's coming down with something.

When story time ended, one of the mothers approached me and touched my shoulder. My mind raced to think of which apology I should offer. *I'm sorry Hannah took your son's pacifier? I'm sorry Elizabeth stepped on your daughter's blankie?*

"You're so good with them," she said. "They are such happy children."

And, in fact, as I do finally acquiesce to their demand and hit the gas, I realize she's right. They are happy, crazed, independent, shoe-eating, charming, sippy-cup-swiping, dancing, whirling, beautiful babies.

So today I pray.

> Dear God,
> Thank you for Hannah and Elizabeth. Thank you for their craziness and their love of life. Thank you for their dances and their giggles. Thank you for their tears and tantrums and their smiles, their hugs, and their hand-tossed kisses. Thank you, God—for answering my prayers.

*Tracy Rasmussen is an award-winning journalist who lives in Pennsylvania with her husband and twin daughters. When she's not writing or changing diapers, she enjoys cooking, playing guitar, stargazing, and telling stories.*

## Road Trip Remedies (Or Things to Keep Everyone from Going Crazy!)

PEPPER'S PIT STOPS

1. Sing every song you can think of that includes the name of a state.
2. Teach your kids how to read a map. Ask questions like,

"Are we there yet?" and "Where's the next bathroom?" and let *them* answer *you.*

3   List every vacation your family has taken.

4.  Play cat's cradle with the string ... remember?

5.  See who does the best animal impressions (facial expressions count).

6.  Have everyone create and write in a road trip journal. Make them fun, short, colorful, and lighthearted entries.

7.  Play games such as I Spy, Twenty Questions, Lemon, or Car Bingo.

8.  List every state family members have been in.

9.  Teach the kids how to make a "cootie catcher," then play it with them. Remember those fun, four-sided cubes that would reveal secrets?

10. Have a "photo shoot." Stop at a zany tourist attraction or a rest stop and have the family (including you!) hang from trees, stand in the fountain, or just make funny faces.

11. List every animal you've seen on the vacation.

12. Create foil art with aluminum foil. (Make headgear, jewelry, words, animals, and crowns and scepters, or cover objects—like shoes—with the foil.)

These games may sound like they are just for kiddos, but we want you to participate, too! Why not? It's fun playing along—and it's just what a Groovy Chick would do!

### Remedy Resources

For activities that require list making, let the kids do the writing or typing. If you're looking for a kid-friendly laptop, consider purchasing an

Alphasmart (www.alphasmart.com).

🙂 Before leaving on a trip, buy any book by Klutz. They have splendid ideas to read about or create while on a trip. (At www.klutz.com click on "activity products," then "travel.")

🙂 For additional games, go to www.Momsminivan.com.

# Peace in My Chaos

CHRISTINE CASSELBERRY

Would God really answer my prayers? How would he fix the mess I lived in? I didn't know the answers to those questions, but I continued praying. I grew up in a Christian home and knew Jesus not only as my Savior, but also as my friend with whom I could always talk.

I had an almost idyllic childhood, but as I neared my pre-teen years, my parents' marriage began to unravel. As the distance between them increased and their arguments frequently ended in tears, I assumed the role of adult in our household. My father dealt with the atmospheric change in our house by staying late at work each day. When he came home, my mother was often sleeping. That was a good thing because at least while she slept, I had a little peace.

Like the child of an alcoholic, I never knew what awaited me when I came home from school. Would I have a fun-loving, albeit childish, mother or a depressed, suicidal mother, claiming she couldn't go on? One time, I discovered her slumped on the bed clutching a half-taken bottle of pain pills. Another time, I found her wandering the neighborhood in the rain, trying to gather her courage to jump in front of the oncoming traffic.

My mother grew more emotionally unstable as the months passed. Unable to handle her withdrawal, my father became very childlike. To feel better—and find approval—he told off-color jokes and drew attention to himself. My mother, too, became more childlike, hanging out with my friends and dressing more like a teenager than a parent.

I read anything I could put my hands on that would guide me in helping my parents. From women's magazines with their "Can This Marriage Be Saved?" columns to books on healthy communication, I read enough that I become their marriage counselor. I spent many nights sitting on the edge of their bed, using the psychology I studied to help them see beyond their own views to the needs and feelings of the other.

But, above all, I sought the guidance and comfort of my best friend. I knew Jesus was the only One who knew the things that happened behind closed doors in my home. He knew my parents and their individual hopes and fears. He knew better than any magazine, book, or daytime talk show how best to help my parents. He also knew me.

I painted on a happy face to go to school and appeared confident and in control while handling whatever I encountered at home. But Jesus knew the frightened little girl underneath the façade. He also knew my deepest desire to one day see my parents happy and at peace.

Although I prayed unceasingly, as I had been taught, I also found great comfort in the little wooden chapel at my church. With its stained glass windows and wooden pews, it was a cozy place to feel God wrap his loving arms around me.

Each time I couldn't handle the tension any longer or felt the weight of the situation crushing the life out of me, I went to that tiny chapel.

Walking up and down the aisles, I'd talk out loud to Jesus. Sometimes I would tell him about my day and how over-whelmed I felt. I shared my hope that something I said to my parents could somehow make a difference. Often, I would even yell at God, pouring my heart out to him, knowing he was big enough to handle my frustrations and anger.

I always ended my chapel time by thanking him for faith-fully being there and for hearing my prayers. I knew he was working on the answer to my prayers even though things didn't change. How did I know this? I just did, deep in my heart. Maybe it was more of a hope, a *desperate* hope because there didn't seem to be much hope in anything else.

One night, as a raging storm brewed outside, I sat again in my chapel paradise and poured my heart out to God. "I don't know how much more I can take. You know my heart and what I desire. I need you to take this pain and heal this mess I live in." As my tears turned to sobs, a peace I'd never expe-rienced before washed over me. It was as if God said, "I have heard you, and your prayers have been answered."

I knew he didn't mean things would get better instantly; and they didn't. But I knew my best friend was promising he had my parents, the situation, and me in his control. Through that knowledge, I could have peace in my chaos.

Five years later, after my parents divorced and I married a wonderful man, God revealed his answer to my prayers for their peace and happiness.

As he promised, Jesus had been there through the years—healing my parents' hearts, minds, and emotions. By his grace he met their deepest needs for companionship and love. No, the answer did not come soon, and it did not happen the way I expected it, but the gift of answered prayer did come.

The biggest gift, however, came one stormy night. While visiting my childhood home, I went for a walk and ended up at the chapel. As I slid into the wooden pew, I felt a familiar touch. God wrapped his arms around me as he had that night so long ago. It was as if he then whispered in my ear, "When the storms rage, I am always here for you, my child. I am and always will be your best friend."

*Christine Casselberry is a pseudonym for a popular speaker and author with a passion for helping others find peace in their chaos. She can be reached by contacting Laurie or Dena through their Web sites (www.lauriecopeland.com or www.denadyer.com).*

# STARSHINE'S HOW'S YOUR INNERSTATE?

## Peace in the Midst of Terror

"I have told you these things, so that in me you may have peace. In this world you will have trouble. But take heart! I have overcome the world."

JOHN 16:33

Soon after 9/11, the war on terrorism hit close to home when Tina, one of my best friends, called to tell me her brother had been killed.

He'd been sitting in the cafeteria of a veteran's hospital when the news broke that America was bombing Afghanistan. An older veteran in the cafeteria went crazy, pulled out a gun, and shot Tina's brother.

In the aftermath, my mind and heart tried to process all that happened. To be honest, some days I've struggled. Some days I've had more questions than answers.

But as I poured out my grief to God, one of the first verses he brought to mind was John 16:33. As I meditated on it, I realized that Jesus says, "*in me*" you will have peace. We cannot have peace by trusting the government to keep us secure or by opening the mail with gloves. We'll find peace in spending time with Jesus.

# BE WHAT'S MISSING

KITTY CHAPPELL

W*here is that cashier?*
Irritated, I glanced at my watch. I barely had enough time to eat my tacos—if I ever got them—and then dash back to the hospital where I worked.

Once again I'd cut it too close, trying to get too much done in too little time. But I could still make it back to work in time if people would cooperate. I looked around the nearly empty fast-food restaurant. The assembly line workers were busy making tacos for the "to go" window. The aroma of frying beef and spices, mingled with the fresh smell of onions and tomatoes, tantalized my salivary glands.

I glanced around again, but the cashier was nowhere in sight. A woman whom I guessed to be about my age stood wiping the far end of the counter with a towel. When she thought I wasn't looking, she scrutinized me with sad, dark eyes.

*Well, you'd think she could at least call the cashier for me!*

I waited, drumming my fingers on the counter. The woman

with the towel pushed a wisp of gray hair from her lined fore-head and attacked the counter with renewed vigor.

*This is ridiculous!* I thought. *I've been standing here, the only person in line, for at least three or four minutes. I could understand if they were busy—where IS that cashier?*

I glanced again at my watch. *Management is going to hear about this,* I decided. *I am going to write a scathing letter about the lack of service in this place!*

But just as I mentally formulated my letter, I had a memory of Rosie, a former coworker of mine. Standing there, frustrated, I heard her sweet voice admonish me: "Be what's missing."

"What do you mean 'Be what's missing'?" I had asked the first time I heard her use that phrase.

"Whenever you find yourself in an unpleasant situation," she explained, "just think about what is missing."

Rosie smiled at my blank stare. "It's really simple when you think about it. If someone is mean, then kindness is missing. If someone is inconsiderate, then thoughtfulness is missing. If someone is hateful, then love is missing. If we will be what's missing, then we'll provide whatever the situation needs."

I had frowned in contemplation as I chewed on her words. "That makes sense," I admitted. But I added, "It sounds simple, Rosie, but it's definitely not easy to do." Yet I had to admit I admired her ability to live what she verbalized.

And here I was in an unpleasant situation. *How am I sup-posed to "be what's missing"?* I wondered. *I know—I'll just jump behind the counter, take my own order, and apologize to me for mak-ing me wait.*

But God's voice whispered, "Don't be sarcastic."

The haggard woman, who had wiped the counter until it shone, laid down her towel and ambled slowly toward the cash register. With tilted head, defiant eyes, and deliberately paced words she asked, "May I help you?"

My emotional temperature jumped off the chart. *So you're the cashier!* I wanted to scream. *Yes, you can help me by letting me chew you out for being so rude and making me wait!* Before I could respond, however, I again heard Rosie's voice: "Be what's missing."

I took a deep breath. Looking at the woman more closely, I was struck by our differences. I was well dressed and had driven up in a late-model car, clearly visible through the restaurant window. And it was clear I was in a hurry to be waited on—by someone who was no doubt, over-worked, underappreciated, and underpaid.

*She looks tired,* I thought. *She must feel that life is unfair.* If so, we shared a bond. I sometimes felt that way myself.

I recalled my anger that very morning at a physician who had treated me poorly. "Just because he's a doctor doesn't mean 'his lordship' shouldn't treat me like a human," I had fumed to a coworker.

With Rosie's words ringing in my head, I gave the woman my order ... and smiled. "How are you today?"

My question seemed to surprise her. She eyed me suspiciously for a second before answering. "Not too good. It's been a lousy day."

"I'm sorry," I said. "I hope it gets better—starting right now."

She almost smiled as she looked at me. "Thanks. I hope you're right."

I mused as I ate my tacos. *We're all the same, really. We have problems and irritations, we feel mistreated, we get tired, and we hurt.*

*And we need to be nicer to each other,* I concluded.

When I finished eating, I placed everything in my tray and

wiped the table more thoroughly than usual. After emptying the tray and replacing it neatly on the stand, I walked toward the door. Midway, I stopped and glanced back toward the counter. The cashier was watching me. But this time, a broad smile replaced her frown. She waved an enthusiastic good-bye as I pushed open the door.

Driving away, I realized I'd been nurtured not only by my favorite fast food, but also by a truth that nourishes the soul; truth given by Jesus long ago: "Do to others as you would have them do to you" (Luke 6:31).

In other words, "Be what's missing."

*Kitty Chappell, a luncheon and retreat speaker and author, lives near Phoenix with her husband, Jerry. For information about her book,* Sins of a Father: Forgiving the Unforgivable *(New Hope Publishers, 2003), which is currently being made into a movie, visit www.KittyChappell.com.*

## LOST? TRY GPS
## (GOD'S POSITIONING SYSTEM)

For he himself is our peace, who has made the two one
and has destroyed the barrier,
the dividing wall of hostility.

EPHESIANS 2:14

# No Place Like Home

Leslie Wilson

Mid pleasures and palaces though we may roam,
Be it ever so humble, there's no place like home.
> —*The Maid of Milan* by John Howard Payne

It's a scene replayed in homes all over the country on a daily basis.

## [ACTION!]

The smiling husband walks through the door after a long work day. His voice-over: "Oh, I'm so glad to be home. I can't wait to get something to eat and then sit down, prop my feet up, and channel surf for a little while."

His wife walks toward him, also smiling. Her voice-over: "I'm exhausted after cooking, cleaning, and taking care of the kids all day. I'm so glad he's home to help with the kids so I can get a little rest."

She greets him with a hug before handing him

their child and saying, "Honey, here's your son. He missed you so much today."

Meanwhile, the husband has picked up the newspaper and is looking through it.

## [CUT!]

Before we go any further with this scene (i.e., before it becomes a knock-down, drag-out fight), we need to examine what causes many couples to turn what *should* be the best part of their day into an argument: expectations! From the Latin words *ex*, meaning out, and *spectare*, meaning to look, an expectation is defined as "looking forward to an event as about to happen." Herein lies the potential for conflict.

The husband has one expectation of his evening—that he has the right to be a couch potato and to have dinner (and anything else he might desire) served to him. The wife's perspective is vastly different. She expects different things of her evening—and of her husband. She may or may not have prepared dinner. She will most certainly want her husband to help with some (or all) of her evening tasks: cleaning up after dinner, playing with the children, helping them with their homework, bathing them, and putting them to bed. Even a person who lacks common sense can see the makings of a nasty and difficult conflict if the situation is left unchecked. So, what can be done about it? The answer is *communication*.

Do you know what your husband wants most when he gets home? I thought I did. I thought Bret (somewhat of a classic, 1950s, "Ward Cleaver" dad) wanted me to have dinner fixed and the house reasonably tidy when he walked through the door in the evenings. I couldn't have been more wrong. That's not to say he didn't like those things. But neither were they the most important things to him.

Several years ago I attended a seminar for young mothers. The format for that particular meeting included a panel of "experts" participating in a Q&A session. Five dads, ranging in age from twenty-five to forty-five, with children of varying ages, made up our panel. Fatherhood made them experts, and they had volunteered—or more likely had been volunteered by their wives—to answer questions about marriage and parenting from a dad's perspective. Although several questions had been prepared ahead of time in case the audience members were shy, the panel also allowed impromptu queries. The following "canned" question was one of my favorites, or at least one of the most eye-opening.

"What do you want most when you first walk in the door from work? Do you want a clean house? Do you want dinner on the table? Do you want to be able to have some transition time from work to family life? What is it that you want most?"

The panelists' answers shocked the young moms at that meeting. But before I tell you their answers, I need to clarify something. These five men had never met one another. They weren't friends or connected at all except for the fact that their wives had convinced (or coerced) them all into serving on this panel. So the response that followed was even more surprising because it was unanimous!

All of the husbands agreed that what they wanted most when they came home from work was to find their wives in a good mood. *A good mood? That's it?* I thought. That seemed too simple.

But then I tried—hard—to remember the last time I had been in a good mood when my husband came home. I couldn't remember a day when I hadn't met Bret at the door with barely concealed irritation and weariness. I'd hand over our

son, Charlie, and say, "Your son needs you." Whom did I think
I fooled with that lame comment?

Typically I was worn out from chasing my toddler, doing
laundry, picking up toys, grocery shopping, cooking, changing
diapers, making phone calls, running errands, carpooling,
cleaning up messes, *ad infinitum, ad nauseum.* I wanted a little
relief from my harried day, but I hadn't given any thought to
my husband's day or what he might want.

I didn't try to create a warm, loving, and safe haven for him.
More times than not, he came home to chaos—which I had per-
petuated, if not created. Though I wasn't worried about main-
taining a picture-perfect, museum-quality home, neither did I
try to make it a place where he could retreat from the world.

I thought I needed to have fine furnishings and accessories
to make my home beautiful. But though they may look nice in
the latest decorating magazine, such homes hardly evoke
warmth. I remind myself that I'll have time during the empty-
nest stage of life to have a *House Beautiful* kind of home.

Case in point: the Weir family (owners of the nicest independent furniture stores in Dallas) invited Bret and me to a
Sunday school party soon after we married. Needless to say, the
home looked like their showroom floor, which I had frequented
only to window shop! Room after room revealed richness,
wealth, and good taste. Everything was beautifully coordinated,
clean, and uncluttered.

I commented on the lovely home to our hostess as we left.

She responded, "Oh, thank you. We just had it redone last
year when our youngest child left home. Before that we decorated with hand-me-downs and garage sale finds."

My jaw dropped. Though I managed to mumble something
in response, I don't remember what I said.

I wish I had told Mrs. Weir how much hope she gave me as a young bride with a home decorated in the Early Marriage style. As I walked into our home that night—and looked at the brown canvas chairs Bret acquired from a roommate and the orange velvet chair from Bret's mom—I felt better. I didn't have to have a perfect home.

After hearing the results of the dads' panel, I reminded myself of that long-ago revelation. I just needed to concentrate on making it warm and cozy for my family—a task that didn't require designer fabrics or expensive furniture.

On a recent radio broadcast, psychologist Dr. Laura Schlessinger took a call from an irritated caller who complained about her lazy, unresponsive husband. Dr. Laura challenged her with this question: "If you were a guy, would you want to come home to you?" There was awkward silence on the other end of the line, then a dial tone. I think I would have hung up, too. Because there are many days I wouldn't want to come home to me!

But I'm trying—I really am. With God's help, I'm trying to make Bret's arrival home a peaceful one. Some days he comes home to the smell of something yummy cooking in the crock pot. I even manage, most days, to put on a little makeup before he gets home!

Who knows? If we take enough pleasure in our little abode, it might start to seem like a real palace.

## [ACTION!]

*Leslie Wilson speaks to thousands each year, using humor to soothe hurts and encourage young moms in the trenches. She lives in Rockwall, Texas with hubby, Bret, and their three kids: Charlie, Molly, and Reese.*

## STARSHINE'S HOW'S YOUR INNERSTATE?

### Finding Peace by Saying No

🌼 Try creating a mission statement for yourself and for your family. Your statement will help you to say no to the good things in life in order to say yes to the best. One of the books that helped me to do this was *You've Got What It Takes* by Marita Littauer (Bethany House, 2000).

🌼 Meditate on this quote: "The stops of a good man [or woman!] are ordered by the Lord as well as his steps." —George Muller

🌼 Read the books *Too Blessed to Be Stressed* by Suzann Johnson Cook (Nelson, 1998) or *Martha to the Max* by Debi Stack (Moody, 2001).

# WHEN GOD RODE A BUS

BONNIE SAMS, AS TOLD TO JEANNE ZORNES

I didn't pay much attention to the boy when he got on my bus that chilly January morning in Titusville, Florida. I was tired and facing a thirty-hour ride to my daughter's home.

Wanting to be alone, I'd asked a friend to pray that I'd sit by myself or that my seatmate wouldn't talk. Another friend prayed I'd stay warm—important because I have two rare autoimmune diseases whose symptoms worsen when I'm cold. She also prayed that a "legion of angels" would surround me as I traveled.

On the first leg of the trip, I got two seats to myself and napped for the first few hours. It was during a stretch break at one of our stops when the boy came up to me. He looked about twelve and needed a shower, haircut, and clean clothes.

"I'm going to Oklahoma," he volunteered. "I'm going to live with my mom."

I nodded and smiled and tried to leave it at that. But he stayed near me at all remaining stops. I'd smile at him, or, if he spoke, give him short answers.

When we got to Atlanta to change buses, I waited for the bus to empty before I struggled off with my belongings. Despite my physical problems, I had to carry two suitcases, two pillows, a blanket, coat, and carry-on bag up two ramps into the terminal. Then I had to figure out the gate to my next bus.

As I waited in line for information, the boy came up to me. The way he paced told me he was nervous and not sure what to do.

"Did you find out which bus to catch?" I asked.

"No," he said.

"Well, just stand with me," I offered. "We'll find out together."

We discovered we had the same bus, a "red-eye special" to Memphis, leaving at 9 p.m. With nearly two hours to wait, the boy wandered through the station, always coming back to me where I waited by my luggage.

As we boarded again, I thanked God for a comfortable ride so far and hoped again for two seats together so I could curl up and go to sleep. I found an empty double seat six rows back from the driver and arranged my pillows. When the boy got on, some other passengers denied his request to sit by them. He paced the aisle, then came to me.

"Can I sit by you?" he asked.

I knew I couldn't say no.

"Yes," I said, pulling my pillows out of the way. He seemed relieved.

As the bus started down the highway, he told me about his life. He'd been kicked out of school twice. The past year he'd lived with his dad, whom he had not known before. He said his father got mad at him and put him on this bus to send him back to his mom. He said she didn't want him either, and he didn't have any money.

While he talked, I started praying. I knew God would have

to take care of this situation because I didn't know what to do. I also realized that, without money, he was probably hungry.

"I've got some crackers," I said, pulling out a package a friend had given me. I also offered a can of lemonade I'd just bought.

As we chatted, an older lady sitting behind us leaned forward. She told him how Jesus could help him with his troubles and explained how to become a Christian. As I listened, I realized God was answering my prayers.

Then a big man across the aisle told the boy that Jesus was the answer to his problems and could also help his dad and mom with theirs.

Next, the lady in front of me popped up and said she was a Christian.

The big man offered to pray for the boy. As he began, the lady in front started praising the Lord. It got loud—real loud. The whole bus quieted, and the praying continued for several minutes.

By now the big man was fired up and started preaching to the whole bus. He said he'd been really discouraged when he got on the bus. He'd just lost his job and was on his way home to his pregnant wife and three little girls. But now he knew God had better things for him.

Then a young woman across the aisle told her testimony. In the seat in front of her, a man turned around, said he was a preacher from Tennessee, and shared about his faith. In the meantime, the bus driver was trying to get his schedule together since it was his first run from Atlanta to Memphis. He announced the stops and arrival times over the loudspeaker, then announced that he was a Christian, too, and gave his testimony.

Soon after, he pulled off the road to pick up a passenger waiting in a taxi. The man wouldn't sit down and argued with the bus driver.

"I don't allow cursing or drinking on this bus," the driver said.

Then, to my surprise, the boy piped up, "If you don't want to get in on a prayer meeting, you better not ride this bus."

"I'm getting off," the man grumbled. The driver retrieved his luggage from the bins, and we set off again. I truly think that angels escorted him off the bus!

The preacher started singing "God Is So Good" and after that, "Amazing Grace." Then the bus got quiet. I looked at my watch and saw it was 12:20 a.m.

When the big man got off the bus, I moved the boy to his empty seat so I could curl up and sleep. I drifted off, warmed and amazed by how God had taken over that night.

The next morning, as we all changed buses, everybody said good-bye. The boy ate breakfast with me, and I gave him some money to get food for the rest of the day. As I watched him get on his bus, I prayed God would send someone to him in Oklahoma.

But I knew I didn't need to doubt. God's angels were all over that bus headed to Memphis. They were there not only for the boy but also for a fellow rider who'd come from an abusive situation. God matched her to another passenger who had just started a ministry for battered and abused women.

Oh, and one more thing: everyone who spoke about Jesus that night had never before taken a bus.

I smile now to think of my friend who prayed that a "legion of angels" would surround that bus. Somehow, they got inside the dim and crowded aisles and set off a prayer and praise service I'll never forget.

*Bonnie Sams, a retired insurance agent, lives in Huntsville, Arkansas. Author/speaker Jeanne Zornes lives in Washington state. They met through Bonnie's brother, inspirational speaker and polio overcomer Dan Miller. Contact Bonnie at texastwostep@hotmail.com.*

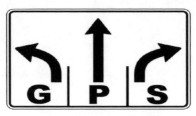

## LOST? TRY GPS
## (GOD'S POSITIONING SYSTEM)

"The LORD bless you and keep you;
the LORD make his face shine upon you
    and be gracious to you;
the LORD turn his face toward you
    and give you peace."

NUMBERS 6:24–26

# Making Peace with the Personalities

Laurie Barker Copeland

I sat in the church parlor, anxiously waiting on my friend to open what was sure to be the most adorable little gift she'd ever laid eyes on. Twenty-five other ladies sat with me, oohing and aahing over all the bottles, blankets, and booties at Carla's baby shower. But I just *knew* that *my* gift was going to raise the roof with extra exclamations. For I had found the sweetest, tiniest pink pants and jacket set, complete with furry tail and perky ears.

When Carla opened my brightly decorated bag, she smiled, looked for me in the crowd, and calmly said, "Thank you," while placing the bag among all her other paraphernalia. I calmly nodded back, "You're welcome." But inside I thought, *Thank you? Thank you?! That's all I get? Where's the jumping up and down? Where's the running over to give me a giant hug, all the while saying, "This has got to be the cutest outfit I have ever seen in my LIFE!"*

As I sat there in the overstuffed, harvest gold parlor chair, I heard a voice in my head whisper, *Carla is a Phlegmatic. That's as good as it's going to get.*

That was the beginning of a change in my life. I began to understand more, judge less, and gain peace through understanding a person's God-given personality. (I'm not talking about a New-Age-feel-good-astrology philosophy, but rather a God-inspired tool we can use to be at peace with others.)

My husband, John, and I have enjoyed talking "personalities" ever since we received a book on the topic as a wedding gift. We've loved having friends over and giving them "The Test." It's cheap entertainment.

But it wasn't until ten years later (I'm a slow learner) at Carla's shower that I began to see beyond just *identifying* people's personalities. I knew my friend was not a naturally effervescent person, ready to whoop and holler at every adorable baby outfit that came her way. But that day, I began truly *accepting* her.

Here's what I realized: Carla wasn't wrong in her apparent nonappreciation. She was just different. For someone a tad judgmental like me, this was a monumental discovery!

"The Personalities," as they are referred to by the Queens of Personalities, speakers/authors Florence and Marita Littauer, were first coined by Hippocrates. He discovered that people could generally be separated into four different categories of personality types. The Littauers added modern adjectives to the groups: Popular Sanguine, Perfect Melancholy, Powerful Choleric, and Peaceful Phlegmatic.

Popular Sanguines are people-loving people. They're generally louder and brighter than the other personalities. Their lives are an open book, their purses are messy, and they run late ... for everything! (They also like to use exclamation points in their writing!) They are not only disorganized but also entertaining and funny.

The opposite of a Sanguine is a Perfect Melancholy. They are quiet, their appearance is tailored, and they need their personal space. They're not perfect, but they crave perfection, and since life isn't like that, they're prone to depression. Your typical school classroom is ideal for melancholies ... they're usually straight-A students.

Powerful Cholerics are natural-born leaders. Task-driven and intense, they sometimes have difficulty with relationships. They think they're always right, and guess what? They usually are! Cholerics think quickly and have an inner drive to be in charge.

The opposite of a Choleric is a Peaceful Phlegmatic. Their emotional temperature is even-keeled and sometimes even sluggish. These easygoing people have many friends because they don't like to ruffle feathers, and they believe that most things in life aren't worth arguing over. Phlegmatics are adaptable; therefore, they're the chameleons of the four personalities, taking on whatever trait is needed in a group or relationship.

Carla wasn't trying to offend me with her nonresponse to my gift. She probably just didn't want to make a bigger fuss over one gift than another (at least that's how I consoled myself!). So after the God-given revelation at her shower, I was well on my way to making peace with the personalities.

After that day, I started *accepting* what made people tick, (even if I didn't quite *understand* it!). However, it wasn't until I ran into my old friend Christina that I learned another lesson in peace-making: communication.

Excited to see Christina again, I babbled on and on about one of my new ventures and asked if she wanted to be a part of it.

Since I'm a Sanguine, fun is an important ingredient in any endeavor. So I exclaimed repeatedly, "What FUN it would be!"

When she left, my husband pointed out that every time I used the word *fun*, Christina literally took a step backward—away from me. "FUN!" Step back. "FUN!" Step back.

It was like an awkward polka. I hadn't impressed her at all with my "FUN" talk. Why? Because Christina is a Perfect Melancholy. I should have talked to her using words that would appeal to organized, efficient people.

I still catch myself wondering why people act as they do, especially when I'm nosing through a Melancholy's kitchen cabinet and discover labeled Tupperware, or it's playtime and my Choleric friend still has work to do, or I'm hinting around at my Phlegmatic husband for compliments and he doesn't get it.

But then I remember Carla and Christina. I slowly shake my Sanguine head and accept my friends and family the way God made them: their own unique and wonderful selves.

I like it better that way ... making peace with the personalities.

**FAVORITE OFFBEAT ROAD TRIP EXITS**

**Corn Palace, Mitchell, South Dakota—**When Lewis and Clark said agriculture couldn't survive in the rough terrain, they hadn't met the good folks of Mitchell, South Dakota—who built a "palace" decorated with eleven types of colorful corn to celebrate the fall harvest (and to prove the famous duo wrong!).

**Wall Drug, Wall, South Dakota—**Wall Drug is an American success story. During the Depression, a pharmacist used advertising and ingenuity to create a booming empire and tourist destination, all centered on a drugstore!

## PART THREE

# I Can't Get No Satisfaction (Peace with Self)

# Can I Get a Witness?

Dena Dyer

From *Grace for the Race:*

*Meditations for Busy Moms*

My father used to lead the music at a Southern Baptist church, which meant we attended church twice on Sundays, once on Wednesdays, and again on Tuesday evenings for visitation. (Have you heard the not-too-far-from-the-truth rhyme about our denomination? "Mary had a little lamb, it would have been a sheep—but she joined the Southern Baptist church, and died from lack of sleep!")

I always dreaded Tuesdays, especially after I aged out of the nursery, because visitation meant going door-to-door in pairs, witnessing to people.

Gulp. Although I became a Christian at age seven, as a teenager I was hesitant to talk about Jesus. And every week, I tried to come up with excuses not to go "visiting." Sometimes, I succeeded. Mostly, I took part—miserably.

While looking at some of my old journals recently, I did recall one occasion when I shared my faith boldly. In 1983, after a spiritual renewal experience at a Christian youth camp, I became burdened about one of the boys in our group. Eric wasn't born again, and I knew God wanted him to accept Christ. I decided *I* was the one to help him.

So I roped him into going for a walk. Then I went into the spiel I'd practiced during my long years of witnessing training.

"I've heard this before," he growled as I began, "and I don't want your Jesus!"

Then he ran off.

I sat there, stunned and crushed. What did I do wrong? I thought my heart was right with God. Did I push too hard?

Years passed before I verbally witnessed again. During that time, I decided I'd let my light shine through my actions and allow people to ask me questions if they wanted the joy and peace I had. But no one ever asked.

As I read the Eric story in my old journal, I ran across the camp's motto: "Successful witnessing is sharing Christ through the power of the Holy Spirit and leaving the results to God." That resonated with me, since I still don't know what became of Eric.

Over several years of being a nonwitness, I realized that I wasn't obeying Christ's mandate to share the Gospel with the world. And I began to look for opportunities to talk about Jesus in a natural way.

I still don't witness as much as I should. But of those times when I have been faithful to share, often I've seen positive results. On other occasions, I've fallen on my face. Regardless, I always feel God's presence and his approval—like a father who is proud of his daughter for "just trying."

Recently, I talked about Christ with a friend of mine. I had prayed for an opportunity to talk to him for several months. When he asked me about something spiritual, I set up a time to talk with him later, at length. Then I called every Christian friend I knew and asked them to pray like crazy.

During our conversation, I stayed uncharacteristically calm—through the power of the Holy Spirit. God brought several Scriptures to mind that I hadn't planned on bringing up. Through it all, I felt peaceful, even joyful.

And now, I'm leaving the results to God.

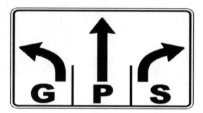

## Lost? Try GPS (God's Positioning System)

"Go to the people of all nations and make them my disciples. Baptize them in the name of the Father, the Son, and the Holy Spirit, and teach them to do everything I have told you. I will be with you always, even until the end of the world."

MATTHEW 28:19–20 CEV

"When you are brought before synagogues, rulers and authorities, do not worry about how you will defend yourselves or what you will say, for the Holy Spirit will teach you at that time what you should say."

LUKE 12:11–12

# WHEN CHURCH CHICKS LAUGH, WE ALL LAUGH ALONG

JOANNE BROKAW

It's because of Jan that I became a Church Chick.

Actually, "became" is the wrong word because that implies a conscious desire to change from one thing to another.

Maybe "reborn" describes the transformation better. One moment I lived in a hardened shell of legalism, fear, conformity, and religiosity, and the next, I poked my little beak out to get a whiff of the thing that would change my life forever: freedom.

I met Jan in women's Bible study a few years ago while at a low point in my life. I'd just gotten some unexpected test results from my doctor, and immediately I determined (all on my own) that I was dying—and probably very soon. Through tears, I shared my fears with the group when a hip, older woman at the end of the table spoke up.

"I went through the same thing a few years ago, and I thought I was dying, too," she said, reaching into her purse and pulling out her wallet as she spoke. She explained that she did the only thing she could do under the circumstances: she had her glamour portraits done.

"I wasn't going to leave it up to my husband and three sons to pick a picture of me to display at my memorial service," she said, opening her wallet and passing the photo around the room. "I knew they'd pick out something horrible and that's how people would remember me forever."

"If I'm going," she added, "I'm going with flair."

For the first time during my ordeal, I laughed—loudly, through tears, and until my stomach hurt. Jan had something different, and whatever it was, at that moment I knew I wanted it.

Jan defies the typical "church lady" mold. She's fifty, but her attitude is ageless. She's as comfortable blasting Boston on the stereo in her SUV as she is blasting praise music in her sporty five-speed Nissan. She's the only woman on our church's building committee (she even has a hard hat with her name on it), yet she's equally comfortable in the weekly women's Bible study. She's hip and stylish without being tacky or affected. Most important, she loves Jesus and is spiritually mature, but continues to grow.

I grew up believing that to be spiritually mature, you had to be reserved and quiet and, well, churchy. No rock music, no jeans in church, and certainly no laughing out loud. I thought the only way I could serve the church was in women's ministries or the nursery—neither of which appealed to me in any way. I was a square peg always trying to fit into a round hole, always feeling defeated because I didn't. When I met Jan, I began to understand the problem wasn't me. It was my attitude.

I had forgotten that Jesus laughed a whole lot while he walked among us and that he'd be disappointed if we didn't relish the joy of our faith. I overlooked the fact that God gave me interests and talents designed to satisfy his plans, not anyone else's. I hadn't yet learned that laughter can open the door for the seeker much better than a somber, judgmental attitude. Over the past several years, as I've become freer in my faith, I've found that my joy spills over as nothing else I can do or say.

But my transformation didn't happen overnight. In fact, it got worse before it got better. Those tests results showed I did have a potentially serious health concern that required major surgery to correct. Then a bout of panic attacks kept me housebound for a few months. Though doctors told me I was fine, I kept waiting for the other shoe to drop, wondering what else was wrong with me. Would my heart explode? Did I have a brain tumor? Had I contracted tuberculosis? *Surely,* I thought, *real Christian women don't worry about these things, do they?*

Fortunately, Jan had shown me it was okay to laugh—at my circumstances, at my fears, and at myself. I finally decided just to speak up and simply confess to the world that while I loved Jesus with all my heart, I was scared and needed help—gasp!— in the form of antidepressants, and that no, I did not think volunteering to help with the women's ministries luncheon would get my mind off my problems.

Imagine my surprise when other women began telling me they felt the same way but were afraid to admit it out loud!

Unlike Jan, I did not run out and have a glamour photo shoot. But I did pursue a career that couples my love of music with my love for writing. I'm often called on to share my story of anxiety and depression with women who are afraid that asking for help somehow implies a lack of faith (not true!). I've even shaved off some of those square corners so that I could fit into a round hole and volunteer to teach preschool Sunday school, a task that brings joy and keeps me humble.

And I credit my first steps toward transformation to a

Church Chick named Jan, who showed me how to laugh at my fears and embrace the freedom Christ wants us all to enjoy.

*Award-winning freelance writer Joanne Brokaw covers music and entertainment for Christian publications across the United States and Canada. She lives with her husband and college-age daughter in western New York, where she enjoys hanging out with rock stars.*

**GROOVY MOOVIES**

**PEPPER'S PIT STOPS**

What's a Groovy moovie? It's a fun, romantic flick to watch with fellow Groovy Chicks, including li'l Chicklettes. These are not your typical meet-'em-and-hop-in-bed movies. These are the rare ones ... the movies that manage to have fun *and* keep it clean. They may even delve a little deeper than the usual shallow theme of love 'em and leave 'em. So invite your girlfriends, including the younger ones, pop some corn, and dig in!

- *A Walk to Remember* (PG)
- *Singin' in the Rain* (G)
- *Emma* (PG)
- *Marty* (NR)
- *Ever After* (PG)
- *Sense and Sensibility* (PG)

## "Hippie Shakes"

Here's a tasty power shake to enjoy during a chick flick or a break from the road!

In a blender combine the following:
    2 cups chocolate frozen yogurt
    1/4 cup peanut butter
    1/4 cup coconut milk (or more to blend)
    1 tablespoon wheat germ
    1 tablespoon protein powder
Garnish with shredded coconut, carob chips, and granola.

(MELISSA PLACZEK, *CHIN DEEP IN BUBBLES*, FAIR WINDS PRESS, 2001)

# I Learned the Truth at Seventeen

TONYA RUIZ

"I learned the truth at seventeen that love was meant for beauty queens ..." Those lyrics played from our car radio in 1975, and as a scrawny twelve-year-old, I soaked them in. I truly believed if I was beautiful, my life would be perfect.

Fast forward four years. At sixteen, I was chosen from more than two hundred girls to go to Paris and become a fashion model. My agent told me, "Your rail-thin body, shiny blonde hair, and sky blue eyes will be your passport to success." *Teen Magazine* even wrote an article about my life: "Model Success Story—It's like something that happens in the movies!"

Dancing, drinking, and dating made my life a thrill a minute. It never occurred to me my excessive eating and drinking could affect my appearance, but they did. My contacts at the modeling agency told me, "You look puffy and tired!"

One morning I went to a photo shoot. The hairstylist painstakingly arranged my hair in an elegant upsweep. I put on the gown the dresser handed me. The assistants set the lighting, and I got into place. Then the photographer scrutinized me up and down, and said, "No. No good. You can go home."

The first taste of rejection as a model devastated me. I felt as if I had been punched in the stomach. On the way home, I purchased a huge chocolate bar and overindulged.

Six months later, I moved to New York and settled in an apartment. One evening, my mom called. "Your agent, Valerie, phoned us and said you've gained a lot of weight and that you're fat. Tonya, are you fat?"

"Yes," I cried. "And I look horrible."

Mind you, at sixteen years old, I had a whopping 120 pounds on my five-foot seven-inch frame—only ten more pounds than I weighed in the fabulous pictures that filled my modeling portfolio. But those traitorous pounds made my face look puffy and kept me from my dream of becoming a super-model.

Weighing in tortured me. By any normal person's standards, I would have been considered thin, but not by the fashion industry's standards and certainly *not* by my New York agency, Eileen Ford. One day, after a week-long fast, I walked into the agency and said, "Eileen, look—I've lost weight." I weighed 118 pounds. She looked me over and bluntly said, "You're still fat. Lose five more pounds."

Easier said than done. I had horrible eating habits. The more I tried to lose weight, the more I ate. I'd buy Häagen-Dazs ice cream and console myself with it. I'd eat a whole box of Frosted Flakes and a gallon of ice cream and top it off with a handful of laxatives. I sat with my head over a toilet trying to make myself vomit. I took diet pills to help lose weight and speed up my system and diuretics to rid myself of unwanted water. I wanted to look perfect and believed I'd only be happy thinner. But both my eating habits and my life were completely out of control.

Thoughts of food and my appearance consumed me. When I scrutinized my appearance, it was like looking in a fun-house mirror. I couldn't see a real image of myself, only a distorted view. Somewhere along the way, I'd lost sight of what was true. When I looked in the mirror I no longer saw a resemblance to Cheryl Ladd but to Miss Piggy. My value, both to myself and my agents, was in my appearance, and since I could not look perfect, I felt worthless.

My modeling life no longer seemed glamorous or exciting. During the next two years, I traveled 75,000 miles as a fashion model. I used food, alcohol, drugs, and men to try to fill an empty place in my life. I explored various churches and New Age philosophies, read self-help books, and consulted my horoscope daily—all in a search for answers. My weight—and emotions—roller-coastered from high to low. At the ripe old age of eighteen, when most young girls have just graduated from high school and are beginning their lives, I decided to end mine. Suicide seemed the only remaining option for me, so I flew home from Switzerland to say good-bye to my family before I killed myself.

I'd been home only a little while when a friend called and invited me to church. I decided to go, and it was the best decision of my life.

During that service, the pastor asked, "Do you have a void in your life? Have you tried everything and still feel empty?" I felt he spoke directly to me. He shared about the Lord and how to receive Jesus as my Savior. I ran forward, knelt down, and accepted the Lord that night—and my journey took a new direction. The empty spot in me filled to overflowing. God healed me both physically and emotionally.

Ten years later, I attended a ladies event at church while my husband stayed home with our four young children. During her message, the speaker recalled, "I took my teenage daughters to Disneyland. While we waited in line, I asked them to look around at the crowd and pick out a woman they thought was beautiful. You know what? They said they couldn't find one."

As soon as I got home, I sat down in front of my computer and began writing about a life I hadn't talked about in years. I wondered, *How can I teach my children to see themselves through God's eyes?* I didn't want them to compare themselves with the impossible standards of beauty plastered all over commercials, billboards, and magazine covers.

Would they realize their worth to God is not measured by their weight or contingent upon having high-chiseled cheekbones? How would I balance that message with the fact that they must take good care of the unique and wonderful bodies God created for them? As I tucked their sweet, pajama-clad bodies into bed that night, I read them 1 Samuel 16:7 NKJV: "For the LORD does not see as man sees; for man looks at the outward appearance, but the LORD looks at the heart."

Over the years, I encouraged my children to be beautiful—on the inside. My grown daughters are now attending Bible college. They've been to Europe, too, but as missionaries, not fashion models. My two sons grow taller by the day.

Recently, I awoke during the night unable to sleep. It was cold outside, but I was warm in my cozy bed as I lay next to my husband. With his arm draped across my body, he was so close I could feel his heartbeat and his warm breath upon my face. Peace and contentment filled me. I realized that if I had taken my life twenty-two years earlier, I would have missed it all.

I still struggle sometimes with wanting to look younger and

thinner. Fortunately, I know that physical beauty is only temporary and skin-deep, but true beauty is soul-deep. God accepts me regardless of my clothing size, the condition of my skin, or my reflection in a mirror. He loves me so much that he sent his only Son to die for me. I am, indeed, valuable to him.

*When you look at Tonya Ruiz, you see a pastor's wife, an active mom, a grandma, and an engaging, insightful speaker and author. To find out more, visit www.TonyaRuiz.com.*

### STARSHINE'S SMILE MARKERS

How in heaven's name have we been talked into buying perfectionism from such a grossly imperfect world?
BETH MOORE,
*FEATHERS FROM MY NEST:*
*A MOTHER'S REFLECTIONS*
(BROADMAN AND HOLMAN, 2001)

# Love, Grease, and the Long Road to Hair Peace

ANITA RENFROE

Being that I was born in 1962, I always feel a little conflicted as to whether I feel blessed or cheated to have no memory of Kennedy being shot. I didn't really become aware of Elvis until he started to get puffy. Having grown up in a tiny, God-fearin' Texas town, I was also insulated from much of the effects of sex, drugs, and rock 'n' roll. We lived about fifty miles northwest of Austin, and we heard about all of that, but no one in our town ever tried any of it.

I didn't become culturally aware until the seventies—the age of polyester and post-Vietnam strangeness that led to the rise of platform shoes and the demise of Mayberry. And interwoven through the fabric of this time was a single issue that separated the country into identifiable segments: *hair*.

Conservatives liked it controlled and coiffed. Rebels liked it long, wild, and free; fashionistas, teased and streaked. Hippies let it grow on their heads, under their arms, and all over their nature-lovin' legs. Malcolm X followers grabbed their picks and afroed themselves. Hair said who you were before you ever opened your mouth.

Historical evidence backs me up. Scientists have actually discovered that the ancient drawings found on the insides of caves (the ones that seem to depict men dragging women by their hair) can more accurately be interpreted as early hairdressing attempts. And if you look at the French aristocracy and British courtiers of the sixteenth century—baby, the wigs ruled. Powdered, teased *out to there*, piled high, and proud about it. The legendary posture of these hoity-toities was not about their upbringing, rather all about keeping that monstrosity from falling off.

But I came into fashion awareness during the Time of Hair. (We even had a musical celebrating it, called, what else? *Hair.*) And hair became a defining issue as to whether or not you could be hired (too long? no), whether or not you were a real rocker (too short? no), if you had the goods to be an actress, model, or stewardess (blah hair? no). We even had girls who became famous for their hair products (Breck and Gee Your Hair Smells Terrific).

I was born bald. Hairless. And my mother has pictures of me up until the age of two with only little sprouts on my head. But when my hair finally did come in, it came in with a vengeance—thick, thick, thick and coarse as a horse's tail. However, in grade school hair was not much of an issue for me. I don't even recall giving it much thought before fifth grade.

About that time, my mom—who seemed to think that cleanliness was the path to happiness—instituted some non-negotiable Hair Rules, and the first—*Washing of the Hair with Soft Water*—was of the utmost importance. We lived out in the country, and our water was very hard. (To this day, I don't know how you can have "hard" water—seems like an oxy-moron). So my mom would catch rainwater in buckets. This magic rinse water promised to bring a coveted shine to the mane. I would lie on the kitchen counter and whine the whole time she washed and rinsed my mop. (If I ever put her in a nursing home, I am going to make the attendants do this to her!)

The second of Mom's Hair Rules was that *The Hair Must, at All Times, Be Out of Your Eyes.* Now, the Beatles and Twiggy made bangs down in the eyes culturally hip and totally cool. But alas, they were not for me. Thus, I recall spending much of grades one through five in headbands. I had a really big head (plus the thick hair), so the headbands always started off very tight. They'd last only a couple of weeks before becoming hopelessly stretched out and useless. Barrettes were not strong enough to hold my hair through a whole day and always ended up shoved into my school desk. (We had the lids that lifted up—wasn't that the coolest?). By the end of the school year, I had a very large collection of barrettes in my desk and none left at home.

As we slid through the seventies and careened toward the eighties, we all tried to appropriate one of the *Charlie's Angels* hairdos. Many of us could convincingly pull off the Kate Jackson pageboy or the Jaclyn Smith shag, but everybody really wanted Farrah Fawcett's wings. My Farrah-wannabe "do" was particularly stellar as it was paired with braces and a flat chest. But as long as I had my wide-tooth comb and a can of hairspray, I tried.

While a sophomore in high school, I distinctly remember the birth of the hair-lightening product "Sun-In." This step up from the lemon juice method seemed a happy medium between nothing and a salon color job. This was also the period in history when we thought it would be a great idea to use baby oil to more powerfully focus the rays of the sun as we baked the day away. Truly, I survived the Dark (Tan) Ages.

I have come to believe that Hair Confidence is one of the issues that separates the Uber-Females from the rest of the pack. It seems that if your hair has got it goin' on, you are good to go. It's the ultimate Trickle Down theory: if you're good on top of your head, then the rest of your body will follow. The opposite is also true. If your hair won't cooperate, the rest of the day is pretty much a wash. We even use the phrase "bad hair day" as the ultimate description of a day gone south, and "wigged out" describes psychotic behavior. As the hair goes, so goes the chick.

Necessarily, as I've matured in many areas of my life, I have traveled the long road to Hair Peace. After I hit the 4-0 marker, I gained some wisdom on this subject that I am now trying to pass to my daughter.

Chief among these principles are the following:

## 1. IT'S ONLY HAIR.

Though your hair may feel as important as the national debt, taxes, death, and world hunger, it is not. It's just hair. And if you think everybody is looking at it and judging you, they probably aren't. Most likely they're preoccupied with worry that everybody is looking at *their* hair.

## 2. IT'S OKAY TO CHANGE YOUR HAIR ON A WHIM.

All right, maybe not the night before your wedding. But almost any other time, feel free to take a hair risk just to shake things up and prove to yourself that you can still flex a little. Just this week I went from being a lifelong bona fide brunette to a platinum blonde. My family is still in shock, and I get a kick out of watching them stare at my head. It may not look the greatest, it may not last more than eight weeks, but it sure is fun today. I'm calling it my "Great Blonde Experiment." I am going to see if people start explaining obvious things to me.

### 3. HAIR IS A PRIVILEGE.

I have observed friends and family members go through so many different stages of hair possession, recession, and regression that I'm aware hair is ever-changing and not necessarily guaranteed. I ran into a relative at our family camp in Wisconsin once. I hadn't seen her in a couple of years, and my first comment was, "Oh, you've changed your hair." She replied, "No, I grew some!" I'd forgotten that the last time I saw her she was in the middle of a long round of chemotherapy and the wig she wore was not really "her." So now when I'm tempted to think ill of my hair, I just thank the Lord that I have my own.

### 4. YOU ARE NOT YOUR HAIR.

You are much more than your hair. You are a vibrant, wonderful, fully formed female with love to give and life to live. If God can forgive you for all the wrong choices of your life and if you can find forgiveness for people who have treated you badly, why not forgive your follicles for their stubborn streaks? They've been with you through a lot of livin', and they just want to be appreciated.

Just for today, join the major concepts of the seventies: PEACE + HAIR. Make peace with your hair. Whatever is on top of your head is just the frosting on the cake.

*Anita Renfroe is a comedian, musician, and author* (The Purse-driven Life: It Really Is All About Me, *NavPress, 2005*) *who is highly original and unashamedly real. She lives a zesty life with her husband and three amazing offspring. For way more info, visit www.anitarenfroe.com.*

## GROOVLARATIONS!

**Groov/lar/a/tion:** n. A declaration or description of something monumentally Groovy, derived by combining two or more words.

**Hiptagious:** An article of clothing so brilliant, others want to buy one just like it. —Lara Haack, LeMars, Iowa

**Fantabulous:** A feeling of blessings beyond belief. —Deb Haggerty, Orlando, Florida

**Modnificent:** Outlandishly stylish. —Denise Modomo, Winter Park, Florida

Send us your own Groovlarations (word and definition) to laurie@lauriecopeland.com or denadyer@sbcglobal.net. We'll put our favorites on our Web site(s) or possibly in our next book!

## KITSCH COLLECTIBLES
### with a little sprinkling of help from Pepper's daughter, Paprika

You're on vacation and wondering what to take back for Aunt Pearl who is cat-sitting. Meanwhile, your daughter is hunting for something "weird" to take back for her middle-school friends. What's a Groovy Chick to buy? Kitsch collectibles!

**Kitsch:** Art or literary works, etc., having broad, popular appeal and little aesthetic merit.

What's Kitsch:

- Salt and pepper shakers
- Water globes
- State fridge magnets
- Playing cards
- Hat pins
- Fast-food restaurant receipt with employee's signature
- Bobble heads
- Key chains
- Baseball and trucker hats
- Lunch boxes
- Coffee mugs
- Menus
- Sugar containers
- State license plates

# Picture Perfect

D E A N   C R O W E

I t's never easy when we moms mess up. But when you *really* mess up, and your blunder affects one of your children, that's the *worst!*

I know I checked the calendar—and I was sure my eleven-year-old son's makeup basketball tryouts would be held at 6 p.m. That afternoon, Russ shot free throws and dribbled the basketball with diligence—up and down our driveway and in between the trash cans he'd set up as an obstacle course. He was determined to make the Division One basketball team.

At 5:45, I kissed him and wished him luck as he and his dad left for the tryouts. I said a little prayer on his behalf and smiled because I felt confident he'd be a Division One player.

Fifteen short minutes later my husband, Reid, called. "How is he doing?" I inquired excitedly.

"Well, honey, the tryouts are over," Reid replied. "They were at five, not six. All the coaches have left, and the commissioner says Russ will have to play Division Two. There's nothing he can do."

Total silence. On both ends.

Finally, I said, "But I checked the calendar. It said six."

"Well, I guess you wrote it down wrong."

Again, there was total silence.

"How is Russ?" I asked, afraid to hear the answer.

"He's pretty upset."

"Are you sure there's nothing they can do?" I pleaded.

"I'm sure, honey." Reid's tone told me not to ask again.

I couldn't believe it. All those hours of Russ shooting free throws and dribbling the basketball up and down the driveway—for nothing.

A few minutes later I heard the garage door and saw Russ come in the door. He looked so sad and disappointed that I burst into tears. I told him how very, very sorry I was. He muttered something like, "It's okay; I know you didn't do it on purpose."

I couldn't believe nothing could be done. I thought perhaps it only needed a woman's touch, so I tracked down the commissioner's name and phone number, called him, told him it was completely my fault that Russ missed the tryouts, and asked if there was something, *anything*, we could do.

Round and round, up and down—like a dribbling basketball—the two of us went. We were both polite. Finally he said, "Ma'am, it's only eleven-year-old basketball."

I said, "That's my point." I'd taken my best shot.

There was silence. I thought I might score. Then he blocked my shot, and the game was over. He told me Russ would have to play Division Two basketball.

I sat on my bed and cried and cried. I felt terrible—and so responsible. A few minutes later, I heard a knock on my bedroom door. After I said, "Come in," Russ opened the door, walked in, but didn't say a word. He just plugged in his portable CD player, pushed the play button, and closed the door as he left.

The next thing I heard was Michael W. Smith's song, "You Don't Have to be Picture Perfect to Be in My World." Talk about a fresh batch of tears flowing! I opened the door to see my precious eleven-year-old standing there smiling sheepishly. I hugged him tight and thanked him.

The next day, I smiled just thinking about how sweet Russ had been—and how glad I was that I didn't have to be "picture perfect" for him.

And God whispered, "I feel the same way, too. You don't have to be picture perfect to be in my world, either. I love you even when you really mess up. It's the way I love all my children."

And it's true. He loves each of us—mess-ups and all.

His love for us is a perfect shot—all net, with no strings attached!

*Dean Crowe is an inspirational speaker, published author, and Certified Personality Trainer. She loves Jesus, God's Word, and people. Visit her Web site at www.deancrowe.org.*

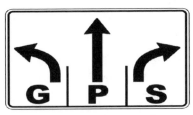

## Lost? Try GPS (God's Positioning System)

[Love] keeps no record of wrongs.

1 Corinthians 13:5

### Starshine's Smile Markers

A positive wife recognizes there is no perfect person. She lives with grace toward others and herself and recognizes that she can be a positive influence in other people's lives without having to be perfect in every way.

Karol Ladd,
*HomeLife* Magazine,
August, 2004

# FINDING OUR WAY ON THE ROAD OF LIFE (OR MAYBE NOT!)

SANDRA FELTON AND KAREN WHITING

If our husbands knew what Karen and I do when we go on road trips together, they wouldn't let us out of the house. We don't mean to get in trouble. We even try not to. Really!

Simply put, the problem is this: we get lost, badly and consistently, on road trips. When we first started traveling together, Karen confessed up front that she was "directionally challenged." I thought I was capable. But I soon learned this was not the case.

The first time we got lost, we thought it was an isolated incident. Several trips later, we have decided it is a chronic condition. We've gotten lost on major highways, back roads, and city streets. We're not picky. You build it—we'll get lost on it.

Our adventures haven't been for naught. We've actually learned some good lessons about life from our misadventures.

*First, it's not always our fault.* Sometimes road signs are totally inadequate. They need to be larger, spaced closer, and better placed. I call on sign makers everywhere to upgrade their products so Karen and I won't keep getting mixed up.

Once I had (unfortunately) scheduled a radio interview during a drive to a meeting with an editor. Karen asked me to tell her the exit to look for ahead of time. Alas, that exit did not exist, and she couldn't interrupt me. She also feared stopping because it might unnerve me as I spoke to a radio audience.

When I hung up, we discovered we'd overshot the mark and had to retrace our path.

Another time we saw our exit sign (which was, of course, not well placed), but Karen was in the wrong lane and surrounded by heavy traffic. We couldn't move over and zoomed beyond the exit.

Still another time—and you can't fault us for this, either—a plane crashed on the expressway and caused a detour that, of course, threw us into unknown territory—again.

*Second, sometimes it is our fault.* As I've said, we *both* have a terrible sense of direction. My fisherman husband can't understand this. "Just look at the sun," he says.

Ha! I tried that the last time we got lost. I said, "Let's look for the sun's setting shadow. There it is! That must be west!" Karen politely informed me I was actually looking at the shadow from a streetlight, which was not really helpful.

Ah, but the maps should help, you say. Not so fast! We're not very good at maps, either. Have you ever noticed that when you read a map, you turn it backward to read it? I have to hold it up to my chest and look down on it to see which way the streets go. Karen, who is usually driving, doesn't have to do this, but she has her eyes on the road and it's hard for her to read the maps.

Knowing our weakness, we've developed certain compensations. We ask people for verbal directions and write them down. We get maps *and* computer point-to-point printouts. And we really, really attempt to use them.

We've learned to add time for detours so we don't arrive late. And we maintain a good sense of humor that keeps us laughing instead of fighting.

Hope springs eternal for Karen and me. We won't give up! We've assessed our situation and made plans for navigational success on future trips.

In fact—and this is a big step for us—we've decided to pay more "moment by moment" attention to road signs from now on. No more reading interesting articles to Karen while in danger zones. No more fiddling with light switches when I should be checking street signs and the directions on the map.

Being insightful folk, the analogies of our situation did not escape us. Life has often been compared to a journey. Remember when Jesus spoke of the broad way to destruction and the narrow way to life?

Indeed, life (like a road trip) offers us daily direction decisions. Choosing wrongly can lead us to trouble, especially if we end up in dangerous neighborhoods. We see this in our own lives. We see it in the lives of others.

Often things are not within our control—like the plane landing on the highway. We can prepare ourselves by knowing alternatives and trusting the Lord that these things happen for a reason. And who knows? The detour may bring us interesting experiences!

Our real hope lies in preparing ourselves *ahead of time* by studying and committing to the master roadmap for life. The Bible offers godly direction from the One who knows our weaknesses and the roads ahead of us.

Finally—and nothing else works unless we do this—we need to pay very close attention to the road map we've been given. Having the directions in hand does not work unless we apply God's Word to our lives.

The next time Karen and I cast off on another adventure, we think we'll do better. Our goal is to make it from one point to another as wisely and efficiently as possible. We acknowledge our problems. We know we need to keep those problems, as well as solutions, in mind. If we encounter trouble beyond our control, we believe we'll be better prepared. So we'll go forth with hope.

That is, if our husbands ever let us travel together again.

*Sandra Felton is founder and president of Messies Anonymous, a group for chronically disorganized people (www.messies.com). She is the author of eight books, including the best-selling* The New Messies Manual: The Procrastinator's Guide to Good Housekeeping *(Revell, 2000).*

*Karen H. Whiting (www.karenhwhiting.com), author and speaker, weaves together practical tips, creative solutions, and inspirational thoughts for women. Her books include the Secrets of Success for Women series (AMG, 2005),* Family Devotional Builder *(Hendrickson, 2000), and the God's Girls series (Legacy Press).*

## Vacations on the Cheap

PEPPER'S PIT STOPS

**Fact #1**—You want (and need) to take a vacation. For sanity's sake, if you're like me, you protect your family's vacation time.

**Fact #2**—Your family needs vacation memories and time spent together while the kids are still young. Remember Aunt Hazel's warning, "They'll be gone before you know it."

**Fact #3**—You have very little extra spending money. The paycheck covers mortgage, car, electricity, water, and food, but anything extra? HA! Does the thought of saving anything from an already-squeaking budget make you want to bury your head in the covers? So what's a Groovy Chick to do?

You're not without options. No, you may not have enough money to spend two weeks in Europe, Hawaii, or Disney World, but you can probably scrape a little cash together for a smart-thinking vacation.

*Option #1:* Show some state pride! Enjoy the natural or man-made resources in your own backyard (so to speak). Does your state have a beach? Mountain? Cornfield? Check out the tours in your area. What is your state famous for? How about your neighboring states? We've taken a fun cheese tour in Wisconsin, a car tour in Michigan, and a chocolate tour in Pennsylvania.

*Option #2:* Visit good friends who live within a twelve-hour driving distance. Many of our friends have moved.

During one summer, my husband couldn't take a vacation, so Kailey and I ventured out on "The Girlfriend Tour." Starting at our home in Orlando, we visited the Jensens in Atlanta, the Logstons in Nashville, and the Chaneys outside of Knoxville, Tennessee. We stayed no longer than three days. (Remember the old saying, "Fish and guests go bad after three days.")

*Option #3:* Camp at a national park. Camping inside a national park is inexpensive. (Just don't forget your air mattress!) Each offers a plethora of free activities you'd probably never experience sitting at home, including ranger-led talks. Kids love the Junior Ranger program, complete with a free booklet and a patch for their accomplishment. Unusual wildlife, lush flowers, breathtaking mountains, weird rock formations, and dramatic water activity ... it's all there for your enjoyment.

# PATCHWORK WOMAN

SHAE COOKE

My life is as crazy as the tattered quilt hanging at the foot of my bed.

I found the quilt quite by accident one day while taking a reflective walk around my neighborhood. Jewel-tone colors, partially hidden beneath a rubbish heap on the curbside, caught my eye. Normally I'm not a scavenger, but on this day I felt compelled to forage.

Though the quilt was filthy, stained, and old-cabbage stinky, I stuffed it into my tote bag and brought it home.

"Honey, look what I found in the garbage," I called to my husband. "A beautiful old quilt—I'm sure it's valuable." I held it up for him to inspect.

"You're kidding me, right?" he said, wrinkling his nose. "Surely you're not going to keep that ... that ... piece of trash?"

"This 'trash,' as you call it, has potential, and yes, honey—it stays!"

I didn't care what he thought of me—or my new treasure. I felt drawn to the quilt and its well-worn but beautiful patina.

When I removed it from the dryer, I barely recognized the quilt. A vivid metamorphosis had taken place. Though still tattered, it was exquisite—very old, likely from the Victorian era. There was no definite pattern, yet each forest green and red fabric remnant, blanket-stitched with gold thread, seemed placed with purpose. Vibrant colors stood out against a dark blue, velveteen background. Though frayed and threadbare, and despite the fact that several patches had been destroyed by moths, it held together.

For the next few years, the quilt remained draped over the railing of my bed. I seldom appreciated my special treasure because during that time, I suffered a long period of severe depression. Anxiety and panic attacks badgered me. A combination of childhood experiences, relationship problems, and burnout tangled my emotions. My body, mind, and spirit buckled.

The day I received the depression diagnosis from my doctor, I collapsed emotionally. Though I was not hospitalized, they kept a cautious watch over me. I felt weak and miserable, full of self-pity. Nothing mattered. Confidence, self-worth, and joy eluded me. Even my quick sense of humor disappeared. I let go of everything that mattered, and I was just about to let go of God.

"God—why me?" I pleaded one dreary day. I decided this was going to be my last effort. If he didn't care about me anymore, what was the point in living? "Why won't you answer me?" I lamented. He seemed so quiet. I flung myself on the bed and wept.

When the torrent subsided, I felt around for a cover to dry my eyes, and my hands touched my crazy quilt. When I pulled it from the bed railing and draped it around my shoulders, something strange happened. I sensed someone had hugged me. As if I'd turned on an electric blanket, I became increasingly warm. My breathing slowed, and my anxiety settled.

As I closed my eyes, my hands stroked the soft fabric. I traced the outline of the stitching, as if trying to memorize the pattern. And I remembered a long-ago moment—the day a social worker took me from my mother. I was only seven and felt a huge sense of abandonment. However, looking back with the quilt draped around me, I had a new insight into that memory— and the others that followed. I realized Jesus was in them.

There he was—holding me at my birth, comforting me at my mother's funeral, protecting me in a car accident, even saving me when I almost drowned in the ocean.

Finally, I understood. I opened my eyes and looked down at the fabric embracing me. My life, haphazardly pieced, resembled the quilt! My past was just as brightly hued, ragged, blemished as the quilt's—but God's patina covered it.

I held a tattered end close to my face and nuzzled it. *He loves me just as much ragged and torn, as he did when I was whole,* I thought. I examined the scraps and old rags and fingered the mended patches. Could God repair me as someone had so lovingly repaired this cherished treasure? In my heart I knew he could. I began to believe he could make me beautiful again, too.

My fingers found a loose gold thread, and I tugged it gently, but it remained steadfast.

Could he take all the random pieces of my life and give me peace? A tear slipped. I called out to the Lord and asked him to become my Golden Thread. Then I lay the scraps and tattered pieces of my heart at his feet and asked him to mend me.

My family still does not see the loveliness of my old coverlet. But I do. I love every shred of it.

My old crazy quilt reminded me of what God did and was

able to do with my life. The "peacemaker" fastened all the remnants and mended all the tears.

Yes, my old quilt connects me to God in a way only he and I understand. Just as I won't part with my crazy old quilt because of its condition, he won't part with me because of my condition. He sees the beautiful in me—stains and all.

*Shae Cooke is a writer with credits in such anthologies as* A Cup of Comfort Devotions for Christians *(Adams Media, 2004) and* Open My Eyes, Open My Soul: Celebrating Our Common Humanity *(McGraw-Hill, 2003). She makes her home in Canada.*

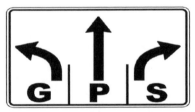

## LOST? TRY GPS
## (GOD'S POSITIONING SYSTEM)

Did you know biblical characters (among them Elijah, Paul, David, Hannah, and Jeremiah) struggled with depression? To discover how five godly individuals faced periods of intense discouragement, read these passages:

1 Kings 18–19
2 Corinthians 1:3–11
Psalm 42
1 Samuel 1:1–18
Jeremiah 20:1–2, 7–18

# My New Best Friend

MARTHA BOLTON

Being a full-time writer has thrust me into situations requiring an extroverted personality. The problem is, I am basically an introvert. I feel a lot more comfortable just sitting in the back, staying out of everyone's way.

Sometimes, though, even when you're doing your best not to get noticed, the exact opposite happens—as it did for me one night in New York.

Crystal and I went to the Broadway production of *Les Misérables*. I'd managed to get some pretty good seats about six rows from the front. Even though we'd be sitting close to the stage, I felt safe enough. Since this was a Broadway play, I reassured myself, no one would stop the production for a little audience participation. (Something we introverts hate!) So I relaxed, sat back, and enjoyed the show ... the first half of it, anyway. Then came intermission.

Allow me to set the stage: the ladies lounge was located upstairs above the lobby area, so figuring the walk there would be a good way to stretch my legs, I excused myself from my daughter-in-law to head up the huge staircase. As is always the case, I had to wait in a long line of women. By the time I began my descent back down the stairs, the second half of the show was about to start.

Fearing I'd enter a dark theater and inadvertently sit on the lap of a total stranger, I hurried down the stairs. Unfortunately, my feet didn't hurry quite as fast as the rest of me. From the third step from the top, I tumbled (read that "TUMMMMMBBB-BLLLLEEEDDDDD") all the way down, feet over head, head over feet. Imagine a snowball (in high heels and a skirt) rolling down the side of a mountain.

When I collected in a heap at the bottom of the staircase, I peered out through the hair that had flopped in my face and noticed the pant legs of about four or five men standing around me. One set of legs belonged to a security guard. Too embarrassed to look up, I merely listened to their frantic comments.

"Are you all right?"

"Are you hurt?"

"Man, did you see that?!"

"I saw it, but I didn't believe it!"

The legs began to multiply as a crowd formed. I hurt, but all I really wanted to do was get back to my seat and hide in the dark for the second half of the play.

I mumbled something to the effect that I was okay, quickly gathered my things together, and limped all the way back to my seat. Not quite the Broadway debut this writer had always dreamed of!

Funny, isn't it, when we're trying so hard to avoid causing a scene, we sometimes end up causing an unbelievably huge one.

On another occasion, I rushed to get ready for a press conference, but as many of you women can no doubt identify with, every outfit I tried on ended up not being good enough.

"This one makes me look fat."

"This one makes me look pale."

"I haven't liked this one since junior high. Why in the world am I still hanging on to it?"

You know the scenario.

Finally, after trying on dress after pantsuit after jeans, I decided to go back to the ensemble I'd put on in the first place. A glance at the clock warned that I was really going to have to hurry to even make it for the conference.

I rushed out of my hotel room, down the hallway, into the elevator, and through the lobby. As I walked, I could feel something brushing ever so lightly against the back of my leg, but I ignored it, telling myself that I didn't have time to check.

By the time I reached the front doors, though, I changed my mind. If it was indeed a loose thread, I figured the front desk clerk would have a pair of scissors I could borrow. So I looked behind me. What I saw wasn't a loose thread—it was my nightgown! Somehow during all the changes of clothes, it stuck itself in my belt. I'd been dragging it behind me through the entire hotel like a bridal train! No wonder the bellman asked if I'd gotten enough sleep the night before.

Funny, isn't it, how when we're trying to look our best, we somehow manage to look anything but.

It's not only our clothes that can get us into trouble. Sometimes it's the way we try to make our bodies "more acceptable." I'll confess right now that I've never been a big fan of exercise. I tried the treadmill once, but my pillow kept getting stuck in the conveyor belt.

Someone recommended I try an exercise belt (you know, those implements you stand on that shake you to about a 6.3 on the Richter scale). They recommended I use the belt on those "problem," cellulite-ridden areas of my thighs and upper arms.

So I stepped on the machine one afternoon, leaned my right thigh into the belt, turned it on, and started to vibrate. Then I switched to my left thigh. Finally, I "attacked" each arm. At first, I didn't notice any significant change, but the next morning when I woke up—to my surprise—my upper arm fat and cellulite had vanished. It had vanished because it *slid down to my elbows*! I looked like Popeye.

I stood in front of the mirror staring and gasping at the image before me. My attempt to look more presentable had ended up maiming me! I found the whole thing ironic, to say the least—sort of like choking to death on a vitamin.

I went to my doctor and all he could do was look at my arms and say, "How did you do this again?" He even called his medical partner in to look at me, too. They both shook their heads in amazement. I think I made medical history of some sort. My arms stayed like that for two years. Two years! But then, one morning I awoke and looked in the mirror, and as mysteriously as they had traveled south, they'd taken the trip back home. My fat returned to my upper arms like swallows returning to Capistrano. But this time I didn't mind. By now I was ready to accept my arms as they were, sinkholes or no sinkholes.

Funny, isn't it, how when we try to improve ourselves, sometimes we can end up doing the exact opposite.

Over the years, I've learned to be a little more comfortable with who God created me to be. I don't sing like Amy Grant (more like Ulysses S. Grant), but that's okay. Singing isn't one of my gifts. My passion, the passion that God fashioned within me, has always been writing, and he has opened more doors in that area than I could have ever imagined.

In Psalm 23 David wrote, "You prepare a table before me in the presence of my enemies." We have all taken comfort in that Scripture, but too often we think of our enemies as other people—people who hurt us or don't have our best interests in mind, people who are mean to us or tell untruths about us. But do you know that sometimes our "enemy" can be ourselves? Listen to our inner monologues for a second.

"I'm not good enough."

"I'm not pretty enough."

"I'm not thin enough."

"I'm too old."

"I'm too young."

"I'm too broke."

"I'm not worthy."

We convince ourselves we aren't as worthy, as talented, as smart, or as gifted as someone else, and we end up turning our back on the purpose specifically designed for us.

We don't feel as if we fit in. And we convince ourselves that no one really wants to hear what we have to say, so we stay in the back row of life and try not to cause a scene.

But what happens? While we're busy trying not to make a scene, we end up tumbling down life's stairs and not only making a scene, but getting bruised and hurt in the process. Or while we're trying our best to look good enough, we end up with a lot of stuff hanging on us, stuff God never intended for us to drag along with us—insecurities, low self-image, old hurts, and maybe even our nightgown.

Or maybe we have allowed ourselves to get so focused on that one area of our lives we're not particularly happy with that we forget all the positive things. Then, when we finally step back and look in the mirror, we see someone with a lot more problems now than we ever had before.

Living at peace with our enemies begins with making peace with ourselves. If we are at peace, then when someone tells us that we're not good enough, we'll be able to recognize that for what it is—her own insecurities talking. When someone tells us we're not talented enough, we'll know it's his own pain or bitterness speaking, and it's not a fair reflection or commentary on our gifts.

When we're at peace with ourselves, we listen at long last to what God has been telling us all along—that we're beautiful just the way he created us, that we have the exact talents and gifts he wanted us to have, and that we're worthy because his love and grace says we are. In other words, being at peace with ourselves means being our own best friend ... just as God has always been and will always be to us.

*Martha Bolton is an Emmy-nominated former staff writer for Bob Hope. She is the author of more than fifty books of humor and writes "The Cafeteria Lady" column for* Brio *magazine.*

## Starshine's How's Your InnerState?

### Questions for Reflection and Journaling

- What are some of the negative things you say to yourself?
- Do you agree with Martha that we can sometimes be our own enemy?
- What are some practical ways you can be your "own best friend"?

# CHILDLESS, NOT GODLESS

KATHY CARLTON WILLIS

My secret was safe. As far as my high school girlfriends knew, I'd reached puberty right along with them.

I might have fooled them, but I knew I was different. As a senior in high school, my family drove me forty-five minutes away to see a specialist. The gynecologist had never seen a case like mine. Shocked by the results of the exam, she said, "It appears you were born without most of your reproductive system."

And then, "Of course, you realize this means you'll never have children."

The news devastated me. I'd already talked about marriage with my high school sweetheart. Needing his support, I called him in his Bible college dorm room after hearing my diagnosis. "What are we going to do?" I implored.

Later, Russ confessed, "My friends think I should break up with you." As he paused, all of my worst fears surfaced. But then he continued. "I know God brought us together for a reason, and I have great peace that he will direct our paths."

And he has, though being childless has had its ups and

downs. During my twenties, all of my friends were having babies. Seeing their pregnant bellies blossom was both a miraculous sight and a vivid reminder that I would never experience a life growing inside of me. Each baby shower I attended only highlighted my empty arms.

The thoughtless remarks of others crushed me. "Maybe you just aren't doing it right," suggested a woman who felt confident I would get pregnant with the right technique.

"If you adopt a child, you will end up pregnant," assured another woman.

But even more heart-wrenching was, "Life doesn't start until there are children at home. You'll never know true happiness unless you adopt."

Perhaps they didn't realize how hard adoption was for us. Several times, we received calls from pastors who informed us of pregnant single girls willing to put their babies up for adoption. We accepted the offer every time, realizing God wanted us to be willing to walk through any open doors he placed before us.

Each time, the biological mother decided to keep her child. But could I blame her? No. And each time the unthinkable happened, God gave us peace that the time just wasn't right for us to start a family. He knew what our future held. Assured of this, we placed our lives in his hands.

I dreamed of being able to breast-feed my adopted infant for nourishment, as well as bonding. I'd read articles that strongly recommended this and described how it was possible. But I developed a breast infection and had to endure surgery that left me incapable of nursing a child. This dream, too, was dashed.

In my late twenties, I developed an autoimmune disease. *Is this the reason God has not given us a child?* I wondered.

Maybe he used our childlessness to protect us from financial hardships. And physically, I've had periods of time when my flaring symptoms would have limited my abilities as a mother.

For those of us who want children but cannot have them, life holds many painful moments. Mother's Day is especially hard, as the entire country focuses on appreciating moms. A childless woman tries to put her attention on appreciating her own mother. But if it's not possible to spend Mother's Day with our moms, or if our mothers have passed away, we feel sad and isolated. Churches, schools, and restaurants all make a big deal out of Mother's Day (as they should). Many childless women simply choose to stay home rather than be reminded of their barrenness.

Through the years, though, the peace of God flowing through my life has helped me cope with even the most difficult of days. In his faithfulness and compassion, God helps me cope with each rude comment and empty holiday. It's hard to describe just how God speaks to me and shows me he has a plan for my life. All I know is that there is a still, small voice, calm and comforting, that speaks to me when I am distressed. This same voice encourages and motivates me when I feel stuck in life's journey.

God did not fashion me by accident. He had a purpose in my creation, and I don't question his intentions. Actually, I feel special that he took extra care to make me different from other women. I have designer parts!

God has shown me that a woman is complete even if she does not have children biologically or through adoption. The dictionary describes being complete as being *entire, whole,* and *perfect.* God is the only one who can make us whole, complete, and entire—wanting nothing. And he is pleased when we live a life according to his design for us.

I've learned that his thoughts are not my thoughts, and his

ways are not my ways. As I trust him with my future, I can be confident that he will bring a good end for me and fulfill his purposes for my life. I try to remind myself that, just like the old television show, my heavenly "Father knows best."

*Kathy Carlton Willis is best known as speaker, singer, and weekly inspirational columnist through Living Out Loud Communications. She moderates the Fellowship of Christian Writers e-mail group and can be reached at ImLivingOutLoud@aol.com.*

## Lost? Try GPS
## (God's Positioning System)

I will praise thee;
for I am fearfully and wonderfully made:
marvellous are thy works;
and that my soul knoweth right well.
Psalm 139:14 KJV

# HIP HOUSE DECOR

Wonderful Counselor. Prince of Peace. Lamb of God. *Jehovah Jireh.* Ultimate Interior Decorator. Yep—you got it. God is the Ultimate Interior Decorator.

And I should know. I'm a prime candidate for "HGTV Anonymous" and "*Trading Spaces* Addicts" (for you novices, HGTV is Home and Garden Television). I love nothing more than seeing a house go from a 1970s decorating scheme to a modern, beautiful space.

Speaking of that era, I'm a child of the seventies myself. I have pictures of myself wearing plaid, polyester pantsuits to prove it. I grew up with avocado green kitchen appliances, shag carpeting, and bright, busy floral couches. I had the homemade, crocheted poncho and wore my tennis shoe roller skates to the skating rink, hoping to be asked to "couple skate" to a Bee Gees' love song. But I know when to leave well enough alone—that groovy decor is no longer "happening in a far-out way," to quote my favorite line from the *Brady Bunch Movie.*

But as well informed as I consider myself to be when it

comes to home decorating shows, I became painfully aware one day of how ignorant I am about God's redecorating schemes. Walking through my bedroom (which by the way, I had just recently redecorated with a beautiful toile duvet and yellow faux-finished walls), I began absentmindedly humming a song from my son's favorite praise CD as I contemplated which home decor project to tackle next. The words rattling through my crowded brain were these: "Come and make my heart your home. Come and be everything I am and all I know. Search me through and through till my heart becomes a home for you."

Then, like a flash of lightning, the Lord spoke through my shallow thoughts: "Why don't you focus on making your heart my home as much as you focus on making your house a home?"

Ouch! I had no plausible excuse. All at once, God firmly called my attention to what he desired of me.

With this revelation, much of the past year suddenly came into focus. In one moment, I suddenly "got it"—all the circumstances, struggles, and growing pains of the last fourteen months. It seems the Lord undertook a major remodeling project on *me*.

The previous summer, I suffered a bout of postpartum depression. My blues were fueled by sleep deprivation and a second-born child who defied the parenting books that worked so well with my first. I cannot adequately paint a picture of the despair and desperation I felt as I was overwhelmed by what should have been the happy tasks of raising two healthy little boys. Friends lifted me up through prayer because my own prayers had diminished to a point of angrily crying to God to make it stop.

In August, the Lord literally took me to the desert. I accompanied my husband to Palm Springs, California, and I must say the search for the springs dumbfounded me. From the airplane, the sight of all that brown flatland surprised me. Where was the water? As I spent my week there, enjoying a respite from the demands of motherhood, I realized that the Lord is the Living Water. If I would just pour him into my life through daily prayer and Bible reading, then I would not feel so dried up.

Right around that time the Lord moved from demolition mode to rebuilding. The design plan began to take shape, and I felt encouraged.

But, just as I proudly and independently forged ahead, the Lord cautioned me that this was no small redecorating project. That trip was just *one* of the times in the last year that God hammered his truth home in my life much like the HGTV show *Before and After,* where the carpenters and designers first tear down a house and then rebuild it over the course of a year.

That was me—the before, not the after. The Lord had performed some major demolition work on my attitudes, thought patterns, and comfort zones. He'd been ripping out the brown floral wallpaper of perfectionism in order to paint a serene color of his acceptance. He'd torn out the retro shag carpeting of seeking man's approval to make room for a beautiful hardwood floor of his love.

He'd even removed that avocado green refrigerator of trying to control life's details so he could bring in a sleek stainless steel model of giving him control. And, he's not finished yet! The brown and orange linoleum of selfishness is due to be replaced with the durable and practical ceramic tile of selflessness.

To tell you the truth, it's been an up and down process. Sometimes I feel it would be easier for him to just start over with someone else and leave me wallowing. It's like the point in *Before and After* where I turn to my husband, who is sitting beside me, patiently enduring my redecorating show addiction.

I ask, "So why didn't these homeowners just find a new house instead of going through all this labor and expense?" And Chris, wise man that he is, tells me that they probably think their piece of real estate is too valuable to sell.

Thankfully, the Lord must see me like that—my worth to him must be valuable enough to warrant such a painstakingly detailed restoration.

And just as the designers and carpenters on HGTV require a commitment from the homeowners they work with, God needs me to take his renovation project seriously. He needs my cooperation and availability to truly make my heart his home.

God wants me to be more consumed with knowing him intimately than with temporal things such as my house projects. He longs for me to find the joy and the peace and the beautiful design he has for my life. His design plan is for me to step beyond the oppressive strongholds—fears, materialism, pride, unbelief—and step into his presence.

Sometimes it's all too much. And God sweetly reminds me that it *is* too much to be accomplished on this side of heaven. But every effort and baby step forward gets me closer to him.

Someday, when I walk into his loving arms on the other side of heaven, I'll be home at last—and it will be breathtaking. It will be beyond any Fantasy Home Tour and miles ahead of even the best design from *Trading Spaces.* When I step into his presence, I'll truly be complete. In my heavenly home, distractions will flee, and he'll make my heart his home completely and forever with every last remodeling project accomplished.

For now, I'll simply imagine it. I'll try to remember to strive forward and accept myself as a work in progress. And I've begun praying that he'll search me through and through until my heart becomes a home for him.

I've even been working on a daily schedule—one that allows for sufficient time with the Lord *and* a little HGTV.

*Heather Enright and her husband, Chris, have three children: Collin, Cooper, and Caris. Aside from writing, Heather enjoys designing stationery, painting, and owning a home business, Bullfrogs and Butterflies. In her free time, she enjoys scrapbooking and sleeping.*

## Sometimes I Feel Like My Cat: Learning to Be Content Where I Am

PEPPER'S PIT STOPS

Sometimes I feel like my cat, who meows at the other side of the door until someone lets her in. She purrs up at me and then turns right around and meows again, wanting to go back outside. She's never satisfied! The room she's not in always looks more inviting than the room she's in.

Are you at peace with where you are in life? Or are you on the other side of the door, meowing to get in? And when you get there, do you want to go back out?

Here are a few ways to be more at peace.

 Make a list of the situations you are not content with. Then ask yourself, "Are any of these situations something I'm not letting God have control of?" Even though we know God is in charge of the universe, we're sometimes afraid to let go of things. If you feel he isn't in control of an area in your life, hand it over to him. Pray for the ability to not ask for it back!

☺ Read God's Word. Begin today making a list of his promises.

☺ Take control of your thinking. It's possible! Literally recite God's promises over and over until your mind is focused on his power, provision, and faithfulness.

☺ Truly praise and thank God for the situations where you know, in spite of it all, he's in control. When you start to grumble or worry, sing (it may have to be through gritted teeth) a worship or gratitude song like "When I Look into His Holiness" or "Give Thanks with a Grateful Heart." Eventually, when you focus on God, dissatisfactions will crumble and an underlying peace will prevail.

And remember, as author John Moore wrote, "Peace does not come in the absence of trouble, but in the presence of God."

# OH, DONNY

TONYA RUIZ

W hat kind of dress should I wear for my wedding?" I asked
my friend. "Probably purple, since that's his favorite
color," she replied.

Throwing myself across the bed, I lamented, "My parents
just don't understand how much I love Donny Osmond!"

I was nine years old.

But this was no mere crush; it had been going on a long,
long time—all the way back to when I was eight and heard him
sing "Go Away, Little Girl." This little girl had no intentions of
going anywhere.

I spent one whole afternoon flipping through *Tiger Beat
Spectacular* magazine and reading *100 Osmond Secrets*, then carefully tearing out all the pictures of Donny and taping them on
my walls. My bedroom turned into a shrine to the angel-faced
Donald Clark Osmond.

When my favorite show came on the television and the
announcer said, "For all you teenyboppers out there, here's Donny
singing the song that has been at the top of the chart for the last

five weeks," I screamed. As I watched and listened to Donny singing "Puppy Love," I felt as if he sang just to me. My sister watched the show with me, but fortunately, she wasn't any competition because she dreamed of becoming Mrs. David Cassidy.

Donny-mania was everywhere; the news showed frenzied fans mobbing him wherever he went. Apparently, I wasn't the only one who loved Donny and his squeaky clean image. Other teen idols like Tony DeFranco and Rick Springfield tried to distract me, but Donny remained my ultimate fantasy boyfriend. I decided I'd love him until the "Twelfth of Never," and that's a long, long time.

By junior high, I was still single, but I smelled delicious wearing Love's Baby Soft perfume. I faithfully watched *The Donny and Marie Show* and enjoyed the dance numbers and comedy skits, but it dawned on me that my relationship with Donny was going nowhere. I felt lonely. My pet rock—though low maintenance—was not very good company. My mood ring frequently changed colors to keep up with my roller-coaster mood swings. Would Donny and I ever be together?

In 1978, I learned that my love had committed the ultimate betrayal. Donny married Debbie! After that, I lost all respect for him, and my bedroom walls became a collage of other teen idols. I wandered aimlessly from loving Leif "I Was Made for Dancing" Garrett to Shaun "Da Doo Ron Ron" Cassidy and from Rex "You Take My Breath Away" Smith to Andy "I Just Want to Be Your Everything" Gibb.

Maybe I was just on the rebound, but spinning around the dance floor, I did my best *Saturday Night Fever* imitation as John Travolta, in his white polyester-vested suit, became my new heartthrob. I felt so alive wearing my tight, shiny black satin pants and a silk shirt that exposed my midriff. Smelling of Babe perfume, I danced the night away to the music as my clothes reflected the lights of the spinning mirrored ball hanging above the dance floor. After seeing *Grease*, I became "Hopelessly Devoted" to John. There *was* life after Donny! The mirrored ball—and the world—kept turning.

Years after I passed the "Puppy Love" era of my life, I married a wonderful man named Ron. He's not Donny Osmond, and I married him wearing a white wedding dress—not a purple one.

One morning, at a neighbor's garage sale, I hollered, "Hey, Ron, look at all these old record albums!" I had a major flashback as I saw all the "bubble gum" music and the Donny albums, which I'd once owned and treasured but eventually lost along my journey to adulthood.

As they tend to do, the years flew. On my fortieth birthday, my best friend rolled back time and took me to a Donny Osmond concert. When Donny, dressed in a black designer suit, danced and sang old favorites, all the memories rushed back, and I felt like a teenybopper again. There Nancy and I were, two middle-aged housewives (among many) wearing purple socks and feeling like lovesick schoolgirls.

I thought, *How embarrassing.* I heard a grown woman screaming, "Donny!" She sounded ridiculous. Then I realized it was me! After the show, other giddy, giggly women lined up for autographs and kisses, but I didn't. I couldn't wait to go home to my reality boyfriend—my sweet husband.

During that concert, I embraced my past and temporarily turned back the clock, but I also realized it's a good thing I didn't marry Donny. After all, I'm not Mormon, I don't look that good in purple, and here's the real kicker: I'm a little bit country and he's a little bit rock and roll.

Know what I've discovered? I'm at peace with my life. And

it's a blessing that God doesn't give us everything we wish for. I believe Jeremiah 29:11—that God has a plan for my life and he knew that plan way back when I was eight years old. I honestly like my husband and my life, except for the days that I have PMS and I don't like anything or anybody.

All this talk about Donny has made me remember how much I love my husband. I'm gonna go see if I can find him. Maybe with a little encouragement, he'll hum "Puppy Love" to me.

*When you look at Tonya Ruiz, you see a pastor's wife, an active mom, a grandma, and an engaging, insightful speaker and author. To find out more, visit www.TonyaRuiz.com.*

## STARSHINE'S SMILE MARKERS

My crown is in my heart,
not on my head;
Not deck'd with diamonds and Indian stones,
Not to be seen. My crown is call'd content;
A crown it is that seldom kings enjoy.

WILLIAM SHAKESPEARE
*KING HENRY VI*, ACT 3, SCENE 1

# A Groovy Kind of U-Turn

ALLISON GAPPA BOTTKE

As a young, single mom in my early twenties, I moved to Southern California from Cleveland, Ohio, to pursue my life-long dream of acting and screenwriting. Assuring my eight-year-old son that living near Disneyland would be heaven on earth for us, we began an adventure that over the next several decades would turn into a nightmare of epic proportions.

I searched for peace, making one wrong turn after another, taking frequent road trips from chaos to contentment and back again.

A two-year adventure into the world of plus-size modeling came out of the blue, and full-page ads for Levi-Strauss, Pendleton Knitwear, and Gloria Vanderbilt followed. Runway shows, commercials, and an agent on Sunset and Vine in Hollywood were quite heady experiences for a girl from the projects of Cleveland, Ohio.

I traveled with a wild Hollywood crowd, living on coffee, booze, and speed—and as you might expect, I began to lose weight. My modeling career ended when I lost too much weight to qualify as a full-figure model. However, that lost weight didn't stay lost, and I would lose and gain and lose and gain hundreds of pounds during this decade.

I remarried and divorced again, and over the years would become engaged to and live with four different men. All those broken engagements and frequent extreme weight gains and losses left me even more emotionally crippled. More than one abortion left additional scar tissue on my body, heart, and soul. I moved more than a dozen times, uprooting my son from every school and friend he had during his formative years—always on the hunt for something more, something different, and something better.

But I now know I wasn't just searching; I was running. Peace eluded me. I hit one dead end after another, never understanding that what I needed was a Navigator who could help me chart a new course and stay on track. I lacked the spiritual balance that brings personal peace.

For a long time I did not believe in God. How blessed I am that he never stopped believing in me. Not only did I not believe in God, I was hopeless and trusted no one.

My life had once been different. As a little girl, during summer vacation, I loved attending vacation Bible school at a church in Cleveland. We did not attend church on a regular basis. Ours was not a Christian home in the sense that God was an active part of our upbringing. But we knew the Ten Commandments, and Mom exhibited the values of a Christian woman by the example she set for her three children.

Yet the divorce of our parents confused us children, as did the subsequent difficulties of living as welfare recipients on the edge of poverty. While a teenager, I felt distant from girls my own age, and I rebelled strongly against any and all authority. It should surprise no one that I chose to run away and get married when I met "Mr. Right." Except he wasn't. The horrific year I spent married to a man whose physical and emotional abuse almost killed me dispelled any remaining vestiges of my belief in a higher power watching over me.

For most of my adult life, I could not move toward forgiveness and healing, a key factor in my eventual battle with weight. I was angry, hurt, and full of unforgiveness toward my husband. I blamed myself, then him, then my childhood, then back to my husband. My feelings roamed all over the playing board. During my pregnancy at the age of sixteen, I began to stuff that painful emptiness and hopelessness with food. After my son's birth, I added drugs, alcohol, and empty relationships to the mix.

Far more damaging than excess weight was my total entrenchment in New Age theology and my unequivocal stance on Christianity. "There is no God other than the godlike power we carry within ourselves," I spouted—a teaching I believed and preached over and over to my young son from the time he was a baby.

For the next decade I floated aimlessly, charting my own course. Throwing myself wholeheartedly into everything I did from work to play, I looked, on the surface, like I had it all together. Internally, though, I was a pressure cooker waiting to explode.

After my brief foray into modeling ended, I began what would become a twenty-plus-year career as a professional fundraiser and special event planner for nonprofit organizations. My freelance writing career moved along steadily; both *Cosmopolitan* and *Ladies Home Journal* published my work. I also spent several years as the playwright-in-residence at a small theater, where three of my full-length plays were produced.

I filled my days with busy take-charge tasks, always on the

move, always on a schedule, always following a list. I filled my nights with alcohol, drugs, and self-destruction. I filled my soul with empty promises and emptier pursuits. On the outside, I looked okay, but on the inside, I was dying.

My life careened out of control as I continually reinvented myself over the years. By the time I reached my late twenties, a time when many of us are just beginning our families and settling down, I had a teenage son who had, in turn, become the out-of-control rebel, causing me to slip further into an abyss of guilt, self-blame, and hopelessness.

Why couldn't I find happiness? Why did it seem as though nothing I did worked out? Why did I feel so worthless, so insecure? The feelings of utter helplessness and hopelessness, of unrealized dreams, broken promises, and dead-end streets overwhelmed me.

How we come through times of struggle often depends on our level of faith and hope, and at that time I had neither. As a nonbeliever, my life had no room for a higher power greater than myself. It took years to discover that I was attempting to fill the empty hole in my soul with everything except faith, hope, love, and joy. Never in my wildest dreams would I have thought to find comfort, direction, and peace in faith. I now know there is a place in our heart only God can fill. I now know I had to leave the past behind and make a life-changing turn in another direction.

Jesus Christ took my broken spirit and lost soul, filled with guilt and pain, and turned me around, setting me on a new course. He filled that empty place in my soul I tried so desperately to fill with food, drugs, alcohol, relationships, material goods, work, and empty pursuits. He forgave me the sins that weighed heavy on my heart, showing me I no longer had to carry the burden alone. He brought peace into my life. He can do the same for you.

I did not "get religion." I made a spiritual connection that turned my life around. I "got a relationship"—a relationship with Jesus Christ. I know in my heart that no matter what we've done, no matter where we've been, it is never too late to fill that empty place in our heart and soul.

There's a lot more to tell, but suffice it to say: my life journey has been rocky to say the least, but I've found a peace and contentment I had never dreamed possible. I've based my ministry on one thing and one thing alone: Jesus. He tells us it is never too late to change direction because *GOD ALLOWS U-TURNS!*

*Allison Gappa Bottke (aka the "God Allows U-Turns Poster Girl")
has taken her testimony and created the popular God Allows U-
Turns series of books (Barbour Publishing), greeting cards, and
other products. Visit www.godallowsuturns.com.*

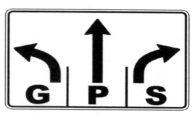

## LOST? TRY GPS
## (GOD'S POSITIONING SYSTEM)

This is what the Sovereign LORD,
the Holy One of Israel, says:
"In repentance and rest is your salvation,
in quietness and trust is your strength."
ISAIAH 30:15

# YOUTH DEW

LAURIE BARKER COPELAND

I spent three days cleaning my bathroom recently. Yes, three days. Now, before you think I live in pig squalor, let me explain (in my own defense) that this wasn't just any cleaning. It was get-down-on-the-floor-and-sort-through-junk-before-you-even-*begin*-to-clean cleaning.

In the medicine cabinet I unearthed almost-full bottles of prescription drugs marked "Take medicine to completion," dating back to 1993. (I guess I was waiting to come down with the same thing again so I could consume the contents "to completion.") In the pull-out drawer underneath the mirror, I found the little eyedropper we used to administer "the pink stuff" to my then-baby daughter, now twelve years old. And in the cabinet drawer, I found a second-only-to-Mount Everest mound of hotel treasures: French-milled soaps, combination shampoo/conditioners, leaking lotions, never-used sewing kits, and those all-important lint mitts.

But the biggest find of all was a mysterious aqua box full of "Youth Dew." The powder inside smelled great, and the name brand on the outside indicated this lovely item must have been a gift. We girls buy nice things for others that we would never buy for ourselves—am I right? I lifted the lid and found ... nothing. Nothing except a powdering mitt and a heavy paper false bottom. From the three holes poked into this paper came the glorious aroma of "Youth Dew."

I vaguely remembered receiving the powder as a gift while in my twenties, but I didn't really know what to do with it at the time. I'd poked a few holes in it, hoping that would send some of the powder up through the false bottom onto the application mitt. Nothing happened—even after I closed the lid and shook it. I opened the container and found only a few sprinkles—certainly not enough to sneeze at.

It was such a pretty (and expensive) box; I hadn't wanted to risk ruining it by tearing the false bottom. Nor did I want to prove just how uncouth I was by ripping off the paper and totally engulfing the mitt with powder, so I had set it aside. I tried again a few months later, as if I could figure it out by simply letting some time pass, but received no revelations.

Fast-forward twenty or so years. (Yes, it is amazing I hoard things this long!) With the dusty box in hand, I pondered the fact that it had been through three moves with me. Now, however, it took up precious bathroom real estate. *It's a nice box, but why haven't I ever used it?* I thought. I poked a fourth and fifth hole in it, but the same pitiful sprinkle came out.

And then I thought, *Why not?* I smiled as I ripped the paper covering off to reveal the soft, fragrant powder underneath— powder that had lain dormant all these years. Grinning, I loaded up the powdering mitt and patted it all over my body. Boy, did I smell good!

I must be a dead ringer for the president of the "Hello,

Anyone Home? Club." Here I was, over forty years old, and I had to wonder how many *other* gifts (talents) I'd neatly packed up over the years and put away, simply because I hadn't known what to do with them. Had I been afraid to rip open other lids, afraid of the unknown that lay beneath? I might have poked a few holes of exploration, but if my efforts didn't meet with immediate success, I suppose I simply shrugged my shoulders and chose the safe way.

My thoughts had probably gone something like this: *What if I ripped open my opportunity and blew it? Would others laugh at my mistake? Would that be my only chance? Maybe it's better just to let it sit there and not try—at least not today or tomorrow. That way, the chance would still be there ... waiting.* Good idea. Put it away and never use it because I don't want to do it wrong and ruin it. Makes sense, doesn't it? Wrong! Funny ... I'd been wrong in letting the fear of doing something wrong get in the way of doing something right.

Jesus spoke of this mindset in a parable from Matthew 25, where a master handed out talents (or money) to three servants to take care of while he was gone. He divvied them up, "according to their abilities." When the master returned, he found the first two servants had doubled their talents. The third, however, had stashed his in the ground *in fear* of losing it. The master was really ticked off and told his servant he should have invested more wisely.

My little powder box now sits on my bathroom counter. It's a reminder of what I learned about fear and that parable in Matthew. God *requires* us to use whatever he gives us: money, talents, spiritual gifts, intellect, and so on. When you think about it, the third servant really didn't do anything all that bad—he didn't steal, spend, lose, or squander his talent. He just wanted to protect it. Doesn't sound that bad, right? Yet the master considered him *unfaithful* because he didn't do anything with his talent.

Whoever said faith is a crutch never experienced true faith. Faith is *risk*. God asks us to trust him, take chances, and put our "talents" to use. It can be downright scary at times! We think, *What if I'm not prepared? What if I'm not talented in that area? What if I can't pay the bills? What if they think I'm stupid?*

What if, what if, what if…

What false questions do we carry that keep us from the sweet essence of being in God's plan? Playing it safe is a waste of time. So take a chance. You may have missed opportunities in your past, but now's the time to make a fresh start.

See what God has for you. Let him tear up your questions and your fears—and then relax and smell the "Youth Dew."

---

## STARSHINE'S SMILE MARKERS

### Were You There the First Time?

**by Nancy C. Anderson**

### If So, You're a Groovy Chick Who Used To

- *Be* a hippie, but now you *are* hippy.
- Have a Groovy wardrobe, and now you have a groovy face (especially around your eyes).

- 😊 Own an eight-track, and now you own a NordicTrack.
- 😊 Eat Pop-Rocks, and now you pop Tums.
- 😊 Have friends who told you that you were psychedelic, but now they tell you that you're psychosomatic.
- 😊 Enjoy the song "Stairway to Heaven," but now you'd prefer an escalator.
- 😊 Dream of going to Woodstock, and now you dream of buying good stock.
- 😊 Wear bell-bottoms, but now you have a *bell bottom*.
- 😊 Wear hot pants to school, and now you wear hot packs to bed.
- 😊 Look foxy, and now you look boxy.
- 😊 Rock out with the Rolling Stones, and now you shout out with kidney stones.
- 😊 Live with acid rock, and now you live with acid reflux.
- 😊 Identify with Haight-Ashbury, and now you identify with Dave Barry.
- 😊 Go dancing at new, hip joints, and now you could only go dancing if you had new hip joints.

NANCY C. ANDERSON (WWW.NCAWRITES.COM) IS A SPEAKER AND THE AUTHOR OF THE *"GREENER GRASS" SYNDROME: GROWING AFFAIR-PROOF HEDGES AROUND YOUR MARRIAGE* (KREGEL, 2004). NANCY LIVES IN SOUTHERN CALIFORNIA WITH HER HUSBAND AND THEIR TEENAGE SON.

# AFTERWORD

So you wanna be a Groovy Chick, too? Well, here are a few ways to let your inner GC shine—and find other friends to support your GC lifestyle.

- Look for bargains on lava lamps, door beads, and cute, kitschy stuff at Target, Ross, T. J. Maxx, Marshall's, and other discount stores. Then find a corner of your home and/or office to decorate—and dedicate—as your own GC space. Soon it will attract other gals who are just waiting for permission to be Groovy!

- Buy "chick lit" novels like *What a Girl Wants* by Kristin Billerboch (Word, 2004) or *Sisterchicks Do the Hula* by Robin Jones Gunn (Multnomah, 2004) at your local Christian bookstore. Then savor them, slowly, while (1) sitting on your sun porch and drinking iced tea, (2) lounging in bed and sipping hot cocoa, or (3) chilling at Starbucks and slurping a cool mocha cappuccino.

- Gather friends to go bargain hunting for "Groovy get-ups" at Goodwill, Salvation Army, or your local retro/resale shop. When you find the right combination of clothes and accessories, put the outfits on and drive through town (preferably *not* in your minivan), belting out sixties' tunes as other drivers stare. (And no, that's not horror registering on their faces—it's awe!)

Plan a road trip with your girlfriends or family members, using the hints in Pepper's Pit Stops to get your ideas flowing. If you can "get your kicks" while driving on the *real* Route 66, even better!

For a low-cost alternative to a road trip, plan an at-home evening or slumber party. Rent chick flicks, have your friends bring snacks, and give each other beauty treatments. Create a theme, such as "Hope Floats" (decorate with balloons, make ice cream floats, and watch the movie—the one with Groovy cutie Harry Connick Jr.) or "Bed and Breakfast" (bring mattresses and pillows into the living room for lounging, watch *Breakfast at Tiffany's,* and make pancakes to nosh on).

Plan a comedy night or poetry reading at your church and invite all your friends, especially those who don't attend a local church. To make the atmosphere less intimidating and more inviting, transform your church's fellowship hall, youth house, or activity center into a coffeehouse. Enjoy the aroma of good java, great music, and God's grace.

Come up with your own "Groovy Chicks" chapter and tell us what you are doing. Or simply send us ideas for a "Groovy Chicks' Night Out." We'll put the winner on our Web site, and we may even include your idea

in our next book(s)! Write us through our Web sites at
www.lauriecopeland.com or www.denadyer.com.

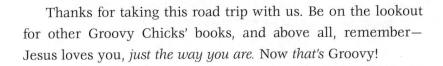 As you find your groove, remember to share the contagious joy of being God's gal! Tell others you're
Groovy only through Christ's peace.

Thanks for taking this road trip with us. Be on the lookout
for other Groovy Chicks' books, and above all, remember—
Jesus loves you, *just the way you are.* Now *that's* Groovy!

—Starshine and Pepper (Dena and Laurie)

# The Word at Work Around the World

A vital part of Cook Communications Ministries is our international outreach, Cook Communications Ministries International (CCMI). Your purchase of this book, and of other books and Christian-growth products from Cook, enables CCMI to provide Bibles and Christian literature to people in more than 150 languages in 65 countries.

Cook Communications Ministries is a not-for-profit, self-supporting organization. Revenues from sales of our books, Bible curricula, and other church and home products not only fund our U.S. ministry, but also fund our CCMI ministry around the world. One hundred percent of donations to CCMI go to our international literature programs.

CCMI reaches out internationally in three ways:

· Our premier International Christian Publishing Institute (ICPI) trains leaders from nationally led publishing houses around the world.

· We provide literature for pastors, evangelists, and Christian workers in their national language.

· We reach people at risk—refugees, AIDS victims, street children, and famine victims—with God's Word.

## Word Power, God's Power

Faith Kidz, RiverOak, Honor, Life Journey, Victor, NexGen — every time you purchase a book produced by Cook Communications Ministries, you not only meet a vital personal need in your life or in the life of someone you love, but you're also a part of ministering to José in Colombia, Humberto in Chile, Gousa in India, or Lidiane in Brazil. You help make it possible for a pastor in China, a child in Peru, or a mother in West Africa to enjoy a life-changing book. And because you helped, children and adults around the world are learning God's Word and walking in his ways.

Thank you for your partnership in helping to disciple the world. May God bless you with the power of his Word in your life.

*For more information about our international ministries, visit www.ccmi.org.*